RECIPES
FROM A
FRENCH
COUNTRY
KITCHEN

RECIPES
FROM A
FRENCH
COUNTRY
KITCHEN

*The very best of real
French regional cooking*

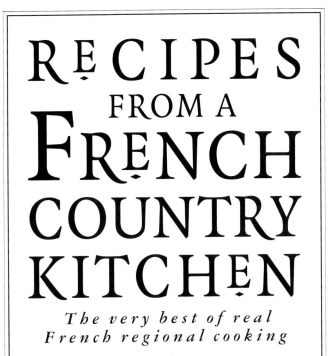

CAROLE CLEMENTS • ELIZABETH WOLF-COHEN

Photography by AMANDA HEYWOOD

SMITHMARK

This edition published in 1996
by SMITHMARK Publishers, a division of US Media Holdings, Inc.
16 East 32nd Street
New York
NY 10016
USA

SMITHMARK books are available for bulk purchase for sales promotion
and for premium use. For details write or call the manager of special sales.
SMITHMARK Publishers
16 East 32nd Street
New York
NY 10016
(212) 532–6600

This book previously published as part of a larger
compendium *The French Recipe Cookbook*

ISBN 0-8317-7308-1

Publisher: Joanna Lorenz
Senior Editor: Linda Fraser
Copy Editor: Christine Ingram
Indexer: Alex Corrin
Designer: Sheila Volpe
Jacket Designer: Janet James
Photography and styling: Amanda Heywood
Food for Photography: Elizabeth Wolf-Cohen assisted by Janet Brinkworth

Printed in Singapore by Star Standard Industries Pte. Ltd.

10 9 8 7 6 5 4 3 2 1

CONTENTS

INTRODUCTION
–6–

SOUPS AND SALADS
–9–

VEGETABLES AND SIDE DISHES
–19–

EGGS AND CHEESE
–31–

FISH AND SHELLFISH
–41–

POULTRY AND GAME
–51–

MEAT DISHES
–63–

PASTRY AND CAKES
–75–

DESSERTS
–85–

GLOSSARY
–94–

INDEX
–95–

INTRODUCTION

Country cooking is the simple, tasty food served in homes and small family restaurants throughout France. It is not without refinement, nor is it plain, but the food itself is uncontrived, uncomplicated and full of flavor. The French gastronome Curnonsky's definition of cuisine, "when things taste of themselves", is a good description of French country cooking.

In France, the country kitchen reflects the seasons. The simpler the preparation of food is, the more flavorful the ingredients must be, and fresh seasonal ingredients are the foundation of country cooking. This fundamentally satisfying way of eating provides the opportunity to savor each vegetable and fruit as it comes to maturity, from early asparagus and strawberries to late summer pumpkins. It allows us to anticipate the enjoyment of pheasant and mallard with the arrival of the shooting season, to appreciate the taste and texture of summer shellfish and to await the first spring lamb.

Traditional recipes often combine foods that are ripe at the same time – like Brussels sprouts and chestnuts, zucchini and tomatoes, peaches and raspberries. The observance of nature's calendar heightens the pleasure of eating and ensures that ingredients are at their prime.

The roots of country cooking are in the land. Not so much rustic as rural, this kind of food reflects the products of the place and makes the most of them in time-honored ways. Because country cooking is based on what produce is available locally, the repertoire varies from one part of France to another.

Think of the differences in the culinary palette between the regions of Normandy and Provence. Norman cooking relies

on its renowned cream and butter, while in the south of France, olive oil is more often used. In Burgundy, beef stew is made with the local wine, but a Provençal version features tomatoes. As the ingredients change, so does the food. The common factor in all regions is the pride in local products and in preserving provincial traditions. The country kitchen is a celebration of traditional rural ways.

In rural life, nothing is wasted.

The French pride themselves on cooking with the freshest and best ingredients, like these eggs on a Breton stall (above). Shrimps netted by a fisherman (right) are likely to be eaten within a day.

Frugality has been the inspiration for much that we appreciate in country cooking: making tarts, jams and compotes with fruit from the orchard, drying onions and garlic in the rafters of the barn, curing or smoking the meat after

butchering a pig to provide food through the winter, preserving goose or duck in its own fat. In the country, wild mushrooms are not a luxury – they are free for the taking, as are rabbits and other furred and feathered game!

Products, such as olive oil pressed in ancient mills, local cheeses made traditionally by hand, bread baked in wood-fired ovens, butter churned from rich cream, are staples of the country table. The kitchen garden provides a constant supply of vegetables and herbs, changing throughout the year. Living close to the land in this way is something farmers take for granted and city dwellers have

to cultivate, and sometimes pay a premium for, but the result is honest, wholesome, and, of course, flavorful food.

Country cooking has always been the province of the people rather than of a professional elite. The development of a refined palate is not limited to those who dine regularly in starred restaurants. Universally characteristic of the French is their critical regard for food, their appreciation of fine, fresh ingredients properly prepared and cooked. This includes a recognition of the distinctiveness of products grown in certain regions and an acknowledgement

of the care and attention devoted to their propagation. Such a demanding attitude is equally applicable to country food as to *haute cuisine*, perhaps more so.

Today the "real" food of France is still more likely to be found in rural areas, where people are not besieged with fast food franchises or fleeting culinary fads, and the internationalization common to capital cities has been avoided. Country inns, farmhouses offering accommodation and family-run village restaurants and hotels are bastions of honest, authentic French food. Shops selling ready-prepared food – *charcuteries, traiteurs* and *boulangeries* – also play a key role in carrying on the traditions of old-fashioned country cooking. Since most people have less time to cook nowadays, even those living far from urban areas, family meals at home are simpler. Increasingly, these sources of traditional country cooking are becoming essential to the preservation of regional recipes.

Like any cuisine, French country cooking evolves with new ingredients and ideas – perhaps lighter, more modern interpretations of some traditional recipes or the adoption of regional vegetables in new areas. Improved agricultural technology and transport have extended the seasons for most fresh produce and widespread travel has broadened the horizons of many people, making them open to different ways of eating. But the principles of country cooking have not changed. Fine seasonal food, prepared with a reverence for its quality, is still the foundation.

Essentially, country cooking is simple, satisfying food consumed with conviviality, and this selection of splendid authentic recipes will enable you to enjoy and share the traditions of the French country kitchen.

SOUPS
AND
SALADS

Universally satisfying, soup is a focal point of
French country cooking. It is a traditional first
course in farmhouse kitchens and small family
bistros, providing the perfect way to enjoy
seasonal produce such as young garden
vegetables or stretch special ingredients
like wild mushrooms.

Salads, too, star in country fare. They make a
refreshing beginning to a robust meal in
winter, or in warmer weather, make an
excellent light lunch. Alternatively, a simple
salad of mixed leaves from the kitchen garden
dressed with a light, well balanced vinaigrette is
often served after the main course, as a day
without salad would seem incomplete.

FRENCH ONION SOUP

Soupe à l'Oignon Gratinée

In France, this standard bistro fare is served so frequently, it is simply referred to as gratinée.

SERVES 6–8

1 tbsp butter
2 tbsp olive oil
4 large onions (about 1½ pounds),
    thinly sliced
2–4 garlic cloves, finely chopped
1 tsp sugar
½ tsp dried thyme
2 tbsp flour
½ cup dry white wine
8 cups chicken or beef broth
2 tbsp brandy (optional)
6–8 thick slices French bread, toasted
1 garlic clove
12 ounces Swiss cheese, grated

1 ▼ In a large heavy saucepan or flameproof casserole, heat the butter and oil over medium-high heat. Add the onions and cook for 10–12 minutes until they are softened and beginning to brown. Add the garlic, sugar and thyme and continue cooking over medium heat for 30–35 minutes until the onions are well browned, stirring frequently.

2 ▲ Sprinkle over the flour and stir until well blended. Stir in the white wine and broth and bring to a boil. Skim off any foam that rises to the surface, then reduce the heat and simmer gently for 45 minutes. Stir in the brandy, if using.

3 ▲ Preheat the broiler. Rub each slice of toasted French bread with the garlic clove. Place six or eight ovenproof soup bowls on a baking sheet and fill about three-quarters full with the onion soup.

4 ▲ Float a piece of toast in each bowl. Top with grated cheese, dividing it evenly, and broil about 6 inches from the heat for about 3–4 minutes until the cheese begins to melt and bubble.

WILD MUSHROOM SOUP · *Velouté de Champignons Sauvages*

In France, many people pick their own wild mushrooms, taking them to a pharmacist to be checked before using them in all sorts of delicious dishes. The dried mushrooms bring an earthy flavor to this soup, but use 6 ounces fresh wild mushrooms instead when available.

SERVES 6–8

1 ounce dried wild mushrooms, such as
    morels, cèpes or porcini
6 cups chicken broth
2 tbsp butter
2 onions, coarsely chopped
2 garlic cloves, chopped
2 pounds button or other cultivated
    mushrooms, trimmed and sliced
½ tsp dried thyme
¼ tsp ground nutmeg
2–3 tbsp flour
½ cup Madeira or dry sherry
½ cup crème fraîche or
    sour cream
salt and freshly ground black pepper
snipped fresh chives, to garnish

1 ▲ Put the dried mushrooms in a strainer and rinse well under cold running water, shaking to remove as much sand as possible. Place them in a saucepan with 1 cup of the broth and bring to a boil over medium-high heat. Remove the pan from the heat and set aside for 30–40 minutes to soak.

COOK'S TIP

Serve the soup with a little extra cream swirled on top, if you like.

2 Meanwhile, in a large heavy saucepan or flameproof casserole, melt the butter over medium-high heat. Add the onions and cook for 5–7 minutes until they are well softened and just golden.

3 ▲ Stir in the garlic and fresh mushrooms and cook for 4–5 minutes until they begin to soften, then add the salt and pepper, thyme and nutmeg and sprinkle over the flour. Cook for 3–5 minutes, stirring frequently, until blended.

4 ▲ Add the Madeira or sherry, the remaining chicken broth, the dried mushrooms and their soaking liquid and cook, covered, over medium heat for 30–40 minutes until the mushrooms are very tender.

5 Purée the soup in batches in a blender or food processor. Strain it back into the saucepan, pressing firmly to force the purée through the sieve. Stir in the crème fraîche or sour cream and sprinkle with the snipped chives just before serving.

PROVENÇAL VEGETABLE SOUP *Soupe au Pistou*

This satisfying soup captures all the flavors of a summer in Provence. The basil and garlic purée, pistou, *gives it extra color and a wonderful aroma – so don't omit it.*

SERVES 6–8

*1½ cups fresh fava beans, shelled,
  or ¾ cup dried navy beans,
  soaked overnight*
½ tsp dried herbes de Provence
2 garlic cloves, finely chopped
1 tbsp olive oil
1 onion, finely chopped
2 small or 1 large leek, finely sliced
1 celery stalk, finely sliced
2 carrots, finely diced
2 small potatoes, finely diced
4 ounces green beans
5 cups water
2 small zucchini, finely chopped
*3 medium tomatoes, peeled, seeded and
  finely chopped*
*1 cup shelled garden peas, fresh
  or frozen*
*handful of spinach leaves, cut into thin
  ribbons*
salt and freshly ground black pepper
sprigs of fresh basil, to garnish
FOR THE PISTOU
1 or 2 garlic cloves, finely chopped
½ cup (packed) basil leaves
4 tbsp grated Parmesan cheese
4 tbsp extra virgin olive oil

1 ▲ To make the *pistou*, put the garlic, basil and Parmesan cheese in a food processor and process until smooth, scraping down the sides once. With the machine running, slowly add the olive oil through the feed tube. Or, alternatively, pound the garlic, basil and cheese in a mortar and pestle and stir in the oil.

2 ▲ To make the soup, if using dried navy beans, place them in a saucepan and cover with water. Boil vigorously for 10 minutes and drain. Place the parboiled beans, or fresh beans if using, in a saucepan with the herbes de Provence and one of the garlic cloves. Add water to cover by 1 inch. Bring to the boil, reduce the heat and simmer over a medium-low heat until tender, about 10 minutes for fresh beans and about 1 hour for dried beans. Set aside in the cooking liquid.

3 ▲ In a large saucepan or flameproof casserole heat the oil. Add the onion and leeks, and cook for 5 minutes, stirring occasionally, until the onion just softens.

COOK'S TIP

Both the *pistou* and the soup can be made one or two days in advance and chilled. To serve, reheat gently, stirring occasionally.

4 ▲ Add the celery, carrots and the other garlic clove and cook, covered, for 10 minutes, stirring.

5 ▲ Add the potatoes, green beans and water, then season lightly with salt and pepper. Bring to a boil, skimming any foam that rises to the surface, then reduce the heat, cover and simmer gently for 10 minutes.

6 ▲ Add the zucchini, tomatoes and peas together with the reserved beans and their cooking liquid and simmer for 25–30 minutes, or until all the vegetables are tender. Add the spinach and simmer for 5 minutes. Season the soup and swirl a spoonful of *pistou* into each bowl. Garnish with basil and serve.

POTATO SALAD WITH SAUSAGE · *Salade de Pommes de Terre*

This salad is often served in bistros and cafés as a starter. Sometimes the potatoes are served on their own, simply dressed with vinaigrette and perhaps accompanied by marinated herring.

SERVES 4

1 pound small waxy potatoes
2–3 tbsp dry white wine
2 shallots, finely chopped
1 tbsp chopped fresh parsley
1 tbsp chopped fresh tarragon
6 ounces cooked garlic sausage, such as
    kielbasa
a sprig of parsley, to garnish

FOR THE VINAIGRETTE
2 tsp Dijon mustard
1 tbsp tarragon vinegar or white
    wine vinegar
5 tbsp extra virgin olive oil
salt and freshly ground black pepper

1 ▼ In a medium saucepan, cover the potatoes with cold salted water and bring to a boil. Reduce the heat to medium and simmer for 10–12 minutes until tender. Drain the potatoes and refresh under cold running water.

2 ▼ Peel the potatoes if you like or leave in their skins and cut into ¼ inch slices. Sprinkle with the wine and shallots.

3 ▲ To make the vinaigrette, mix the mustard and vinegar in a small bowl, then whisk in the oil, 1 tbsp at a time. Season and pour over the potatoes.

4 ▲ Add the herbs to the potatoes and toss until well mixed.

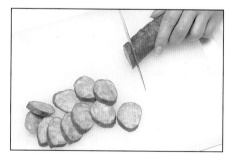

5 ▲ Slice the sausage thinly and toss with the potatoes. Season with salt and pepper to taste and serve at room temperature garnished with a parsley sprig.

CURLY ENDIVE SALAD WITH BACON

Frisée aux Lardons

This country-style salad is popular all over France. When they are in season, dandelion leaves often replace the endive and the salad is sometimes sprinkled with chopped hard-boiled egg.

SERVES 4

6 cups curly endive or escarole leaves
5–6 tbsp extra virgin olive oil
6 ounce piece of smoked bacon, diced, or
    6 thick-cut bacon slices, cut crosswise
    into thin strips
1 cup white bread cubes
1 small garlic clove, finely chopped
1 tbsp red wine vinegar
2 tsp Dijon mustard
salt and freshly ground black pepper

1 ▲ Tear the lettuce into bite-size pieces and put in a salad bowl.

2 ▲ Heat 1 tbsp of the oil in a medium non-stick frying pan over a medium-low heat and add the bacon. Fry gently until well browned, stirring occasionally. Remove the bacon with a slotted spoon and drain on paper towels.

3 ▼ Add another 2 tbsp of oil to the pan and fry the bread cubes over medium-high heat, turning frequently, until evenly browned. Remove the bread cubes with a slotted spoon and drain on paper towels. Discard any remaining fat.

4 ▲ Stir the garlic, vinegar and mustard into the pan with the remaining oil and heat until just warm, whisking to combine. Season to taste, then pour the dressing over the salad and sprinkle with the fried bacon and croûtons.

PROVENÇAL SALAD

Salade Niçoise

There are probably as many versions of this salad as there are cooks in Provence. With good French bread, this regional classic makes a wonderful summer lunch or light supper.

SERVES 4–6

8 ounces green beans
1 pound new potatoes, peeled and cut
    into 1 inch pieces
white wine vinegar and olive oil, for
    sprinkling
1 small Romaine or Boston lettuce,
    washed, dried and torn into bite-size
    pieces
4 ripe plum tomatoes, quartered
1 small cucumber, peeled, seeded and
    diced
1 green or red bell pepper, thinly sliced
4 hard-boiled eggs, peeled and quartered
24 Niçoise or black olives
8 ounce can tuna in water, drained
2 ounce can anchovy fillets in olive oil,
    drained
basil leaves, to garnish
garlic croûtons, to serve

FOR THE ANCHOVY VINAIGRETTE
1 heaping tbsp Dijon mustard
2 ounces can anchovy fillets in olive oil,
    drained
1 garlic clove, crushed
4 tbsp lemon juice or white
    wine vinegar
½ cup sunflower oil
½ cup extra virgin olive oil
freshly ground black pepper

COOK'S TIP

To make garlic croûtons, thinly slice a baguette or cut larger loaves, such as rustic country bread, into 1 inch cubes. Place the bread in a single layer on a baking sheet and bake in a 350°F oven for 7–10 minutes or until golden, turning once. Rub the toast with a garlic clove and serve hot, or cool then store in an airtight container to serve at room temperature.

1 ▲ First make the anchovy vinaigrette. Place the mustard, anchovies and garlic in a bowl and blend together by pressing the garlic and anchovies against the sides of the bowl. Season generously with pepper. Using a small whisk, blend in the lemon juice or wine vinegar. Slowly whisk in the sunflower oil in a thin stream and then the olive oil, whisking until the dressing is smooth and creamy.

2 Alternatively, put all the ingredients except the oil in a food processor fitted with the metal blade and process to combine. With the machine running, slowly add the oils in a thin stream until the vinaigrette is thick and creamy.

3 ▲ Drop the green beans into a large saucepan of boiling water and boil for 3 minutes until tender, yet crisp. Transfer the beans to a colander with a slotted spoon, then rinse under cold running water. Drain again and set aside.

4 ▲ Add the potatoes to the same boiling water, reduce the heat and simmer for 10–15 minutes until just tender, then drain. Sprinkle with a little vinegar and olive oil and a spoonful of the vinaigrette.

5 ▲ Arrange the lettuce on a platter, top with the tomatoes, cucumber and pepper, then add the green beans and potatoes.

6 ▲ Arrange the eggs, olives, tuna and anchovies on top and garnish with the basil leaves. Drizzle with the remaining vinaigrette and serve with garlic croûtons.

VEGETABLES AND SIDE DISHES

The colorful array of seasonal vegetables found in markets throughout France plays a key role in country cooking. Garden vegetables, woodland mushrooms, lentils and grains offer infinite variety throughout the year. The French often cook fresh young vegetables such as peas, beans and carrots quite simply – boiling or steaming them and serving with a little butter and seasoning. Some vegetables lend themselves to more elaborate presentation, and the following recipes are perfect to serve as side dishes with roast or broiled meat, poultry or game, or as part of a vegetarian meal. Whether plain or fancy, French country cooking makes the most of vegetables.

FESTIVE BRUSSELS SPROUTS

Choux de Bruxelles Braisées

In this recipe Brussels sprouts are braised with chestnuts, which are very popular in France.

SERVES 4–6

½ pound chestnuts
½ cup milk
4 cups small tender Brussels sprouts
2 tbsp butter
1 shallot, finely chopped
2–3 tbsp dry white wine or water

COOK'S TIP

Fresh chestnuts have a wonderful texture and flavor, but bottled or canned unsweetened whole chestnuts make an adequate substitute. They are available in specialty stores and many supermarkets.

---

1 Using a small knife, score a cross in the base of each chestnut. Over medium-high heat, bring a saucepan of water to a boil, drop in the chestnuts and boil for 6–8 minutes. Remove the pan from the heat.

2 ▲ Using a slotted spoon, remove a few chestnuts, leaving the others immersed in water until ready to peel. Hold in a paper towel, remove the outer shell with a knife and then peel off the inner skin.

3 Rinse the pan, return the peeled chestnuts to the pan and add the milk. Add enough water to completely cover the chestnuts. Simmer over medium heat for 12–15 minutes until the chestnuts are just tender. Drain and set aside.

4 Remove any wilted or yellow leaves from the Brussels sprouts. Trim the root end but leave intact or the leaves will separate. Using a small knife, score a cross in the base of each sprout so they cook evenly.

5 ▲ In a large heavy frying pan, melt the butter over medium heat. Stir in the chopped shallot and cook for 1–2 minutes until just softened, then add the Brussels sprouts and wine or water. Cook, covered, over medium heat for 6–8 minutes, shaking the pan and stirring occasionally, adding a little more water if necessary.

6 ▲ Add the poached chestnuts and toss gently to combine, then cover and cook for 3–5 minutes more until the chestnuts and Brussels sprouts are tender.

CAULIFLOWER AU GRATIN

Choufleur au Gratin

A vegetable gratin is a classic supper dish in French homes. It also makes a great accompaniment to plain roast meat or chicken. If you wish, prepare it in individual gratin dishes.

SERVES 4–6

1 pound cauliflower, broken into florets
3 tbsp butter
4 tbsp flour
1½ cups milk
1 bay leaf
pinch of ground nutmeg
1 tbsp Dijon mustard
1½ cups grated Swiss cheese
salt and freshly ground black pepper

1 ▲ Preheat the oven to 350°F. Lightly butter a large gratin dish or shallow baking dish.

2 ▲ Bring a large saucepan of salted water to a boil, add the cauliflower florets and cook for 6–8 minutes until just tender. Alternatively, bring water to a boil in the base of a covered steamer and steam the cauliflower over boiling water for 12–15 minutes until just tender.

3 ▲ Melt the butter in a heavy saucepan over medium heat, add the flour and cook until just golden, stirring constantly. Pour in half the milk, stirring until smooth, then stir in the remaining milk and add the bay leaf. Season with salt, pepper and nutmeg. Reduce the heat to medium-low, cover and simmer for about 5 minutes, stirring occasionally, then remove the pan from the heat. Discard the bay leaf, add the mustard and half the cheese and stir until melted.

4 ▼ Arrange the cauliflower in the dish. Pour over the cheese sauce and sprinkle with the remaining cheese. Bake for about 20 minutes until bubbly and well browned.

VARIATIONS

If you wish, add diced ham or cooked bacon to the cauliflower before covering with the cheese sauce, or use broccoli florets in place of cauliflower.

RICE PILAF

Riz Pilaf

In France the word pilaf refers to the cooking method of sautéing food in fat before adding liquid. This method produces perfect rice every time.

<u>SERVES 6–8</u>

3 tbsp butter or 3–4 tbsp oil
1 medium onion, finely chopped
2 cups long grain rice
3 cups chicken broth or water
½ tsp dried thyme
1 small bay leaf
salt and freshly ground black pepper
1–2 tbsp chopped fresh parsley, dill or
    chives, to garnish

COOK'S TIP

Once cooked, the rice will remain
hot for half an hour, tightly
covered. Or, spoon into a
microwave-safe bowl, cover and
microwave on High (full power)
for about 5 minutes until hot.

---

1 ▼ In a large heavy saucepan, melt the butter or heat the oil over medium heat. Add the onion and cook for 2–3 minutes until just softened, stirring constantly. Add the rice and cook for 1–2 minutes until the rice becomes translucent but does not begin to brown, stirring frequently.

2 ▲ Add the broth or water, dried thyme and bay leaf and season with salt and pepper. Bring to a boil over high heat, stirring frequently. Just as the rice begins to boil, cover the surface with a round of foil or a wax paper circle and cover the saucepan. Reduce the heat to very low and cook for 20 minutes (do not lift the cover or stir). Serve hot, garnished with fresh herbs.

SAUTÉED WILD MUSHROOMS *Champignons Sauvages à la Bordelaise*

This is a quick dish to prepare and makes an ideal accompaniment to all kinds of roast and grilled meats. Use any combination of wild or "cultivated wild" mushrooms you can find.

<u>SERVES 6</u>

2 pounds mixed fresh wild and cultivated
    mushrooms, such as morels, porcini,
    chanterelles, oyster or shiitake
2 tbsp olive oil
2 tbsp unsalted butter
2 garlic cloves, finely chopped
3 or 4 shallots, finely chopped
3–4 tbsp chopped fresh parsley, or a
    mixture of fresh herbs
salt and freshly ground black pepper

1 Wash and carefully dry any very dirty mushrooms. Trim the stems and cut the mushrooms into quarters or slice if very large.

2 ▲ In a large heavy frying pan, heat the oil over medium-high heat. Add the butter and swirl to melt, then stir in the mushrooms and cook for 4–5 minutes until they begin to brown.

3 ▼ Add the garlic and shallots and cook for 4–5 minutes more until the mushrooms are tender and any liquid given off has evaporated. Season with salt and pepper and stir in the parsley or mixed herbs.

GARLIC MASHED POTATOES   *Purée de Pommes de Terre à l'Ail*

These creamy mashed potatoes are perfect with all kinds of roasted or sautéed meats – and although it seems like a lot of garlic, the flavor is sweet and subtle when the garlic is cooked in this way.

<u>SERVES 6–8</u>

2 garlic bulbs, separated into cloves,
   unpeeled
½ cup unsalted butter
3 pounds baking potatoes
½–¾ cup milk
salt and white pepper

COOK'S TIP

This recipe makes a very light, creamy purée. Use less milk to achieve a firmer purée, more for a softer purée. Be sure the milk is almost boiling or it will cool the potato mixture. Keep the potato purée warm in a bowl over simmering water.

---

1 Bring a small saucepan of water to a boil over high heat. Add the garlic cloves and boil for 2 minutes, then drain and peel.

2 ▲ In a heavy frying pan, melt half the butter over low heat. Add the blanched garlic cloves, then cover and cook gently for 20–25 minutes until very tender and just golden, shaking the pan and stirring occasionally. Do not allow the garlic to scorch or brown.

3 ▲ Remove the pan from the heat to cool slightly. Spoon the garlic and any butter into a blender or a food processor fitted with the metal blade and process until smooth. Pour into a small bowl, press plastic wrap onto the surface to prevent a skin from forming and set aside.

4 Peel and quarter the potatoes, place in a large saucepan and add enough cold water to just cover them. Salt the water generously and bring to a boil over high heat. Cook the potatoes until tender, then drain and work through a food mill or press through a sieve back into the saucepan. Return the pan to medium heat and, using a wooden spoon, stir the potatoes for 1–2 minutes to dry out completely. Remove the pan from the heat.

5 ▲ Warm the milk over medium-high heat until bubbles form around the edge. Gradually beat the milk, remaining butter and reserved garlic purée into the potatoes, then season with salt, if needed, and a little white pepper.

FRENCH SCALLOPED POTATOES   *Pommes de Terre Dauphinoise*

These potatoes taste far richer than you would expect even with only a little cream – they are delicious with just about everything, but in France, they are nearly always served with roast lamb.

SERVES 6

2¼ pounds potatoes
3⅔ cups milk
pinch of ground nutmeg
1 bay leaf
1–2 tbsp butter, softened
2 or 3 garlic cloves, very finely chopped
3–4 tbsp crème fraîche or heavy cream
    (optional)
salt and freshly ground black pepper

1 ▲ Preheat the oven to 350°F. Cut the potatoes into fairly thin slices.

2 ▲ Put the potatoes in a large saucepan and pour over the milk, adding more to cover if needed. Add the salt and pepper, nutmeg and the bay leaf. Bring slowly to a boil over medium heat and simmer for about 15 minutes until the potatoes just start to soften, but are not completely cooked, and the milk has thickened.

3 ▼ Generously butter a 14 inch oval gratin dish or an 8 cup shallow baking dish and sprinkle the garlic over the base.

COOK'S TIP

If cooked ahead, this dish will keep hot in a warm oven for an hour or so, if necessary, without suffering; moisten the top with a little extra cream, if you like.

4 ▲ Using a slotted spoon, transfer the potatoes to the gratin or baking dish. Taste the milk and adjust the seasoning, then pour over enough of the milk to come just to the surface of the potatoes, but not cover them. Spoon a thin layer of cream over the top, or, if you prefer, add more of the thickened milk to cover.

5 Bake the potatoes for about 1 hour until the milk is absorbed and the top is a deep golden brown.

Zucchini and Tomato Bake

Tian Provençal

This dish has been made for centuries in Provence and it gets its name from the shallow casserole, tian, *in which it is traditionally cooked. In the days before home kitchens had ovens, the assembled dish was carried to the bakery to make use of the heat remaining after the bread was baked.*

SERVES 4

1 tbsp olive oil, plus more for
*   drizzling*
1 large onion (about 8 ounces), sliced
1 garlic clove, finely chopped
1 pound tomatoes
1 pound zucchini
1 tsp dried herbes de Provence
2 tbsp grated Parmesan cheese
salt and freshly ground black pepper

1 Preheat the oven to 350°F. Heat the oil in a heavy saucepan over low heat and cook the onion and garlic for about 20 minutes until soft and golden. Spread over the base of a 12 inch shallow baking dish.

2 ▲ Cut the tomatoes crosswise into ¼ inch thick slices. (If the tomatoes are very large, cut the slices in half.)

3 Cut the zucchini diagonally into slices about ½ inch thick.

4 ▼ Arrange alternating rows of zucchini and tomatoes over the onion mixture and sprinkle with herbs, cheese and salt and pepper. Drizzle with olive oil, then bake for 25 minutes until the vegetables are tender. Serve hot or warm.

Baked Tomatoes with Garlic

Tomates à la Provençale

These tomatoes, epitomizing the flavor of Provence, are perfect with roast meat or poultry. You can prepare them a few hours ahead, then cook them while carving the roast.

SERVES 4

2 large tomatoes
3 tbsp dry breadcrumbs
2 garlic cloves, very finely chopped
2 tbsp chopped fresh parsley
2–3 tbsp olive oil
salt and freshly ground black pepper
flat leaf parsley sprigs, to garnish

1 Preheat the oven to 425°F. Cut the tomatoes in half crosswise and arrange them cut side up on a foil-lined baking sheet.

2 ▲ Mix together the breadcrumbs, garlic, parsley and salt and pepper and spoon over the tomato halves.

3 ▼ Drizzle generously with olive oil and bake the tomatoes at the top of the oven for about 8–10 minutes until lightly browned. Serve at once, garnished with parsley sprigs.

26

LENTILS WITH BACON

Lentilles Braisées aux Lardons

The best lentils grown in France come from Le Puy, in the Auvergne. They are very small and the color of dark slate – look for them in specialty stores and supermarkets.

SERVES 6–8

2½ cups brown or green lentils, well
    rinsed and picked over
1 tbsp olive oil
½ pound bacon, diced
1 onion, finely chopped
2 garlic cloves, finely chopped
2 tomatoes, peeled, seeded and chopped
½ tsp dried thyme
1 bay leaf
about 1½ cups beef or chicken broth
2–3 tbsp heavy cream (optional)
salt and freshly ground black pepper
1–2 tbsp chopped fresh parsley,
    to garnish

1 ▼ Put the lentils in a large
saucepan and cover with cold water.
Bring to a boil over high heat and
boil gently for 15 minutes. Drain
and set aside.

2 In a heavy frying pan, heat the oil
over medium heat. Add the bacon
and cook for 5–7 minutes until crisp,
then transfer the bacon to a plate.

3 ▲ Stir the onion into the fat in the
pan and cook for 2–3 minutes until
just softened. Add the garlic and
cook for 1 minute, then stir in the
tomatoes, thyme, salt and pepper,
bay leaf and lentils.

4 ▲ Add the broth and cover the
pan. Cook over a medium-low heat
for 25–45 minutes, until the lentils
are just tender, stirring occasionally.
Add a little more broth or water to
the pan, if needed.

5 ▲ Uncover the pan and allow any
excess liquid to evaporate. Add the
reserved bacon, and cream, if using,
and heat through for 1–2 minutes.
Serve hot, with a scattering of
chopped parsley on top.

BRAISED RED CABBAGE

Chou Rouge Braisé

The combination of red wine vinegar and sugar gives this dish a sweet, yet tart flavor. In France it is often served with game, but it is also delicious with pork, duck or cold sliced meats.

SERVES 6–8

2 tbsp vegetable oil
2 medium onions, thinly sliced
2 eating apples, peeled, cored and thinly
    sliced
1 head red cabbage (about 2–2½
    pounds), trimmed, cored, halved and
    thinly sliced
4 tbsp red wine vinegar
1–2 tbsp sugar
¼ tsp ground cloves
1–2 tsp mustard seeds
⅓ cup raisins or currants
about ½ cup red wine or water
1–2 tbsp red currant jelly (optional)
salt and freshly ground black pepper

1 ▲ In a large stainless steel saucepan or flameproof casserole, heat the oil over medium heat. Add the onions and cook for 7–10 minutes until golden.

2 ▲ Stir in the apples and cook, stirring, for 2–3 minutes until they are just softened.

3 ▲ Add the cabbage, red wine vinegar, sugar, cloves, mustard seeds, raisins or currants, red wine or water and salt and pepper, stirring until well mixed. Bring to a boil over medium-high heat, stirring occasionally.

4 ▼ Cover and cook over medium-low heat for 35–40 minutes until the cabbage is tender and the liquid is just absorbed, stirring occasionally. Add a little more red wine or water if the liquid evaporates before the cabbage is tender. Just before serving, stir in the red currant jelly, if using, to sweeten and glaze the cabbage.

EGGS
AND
CHEESE

What could be more typical of country cooking than freshly laid farm eggs and cheese from local cows or goats. Although in France eggs are seldom eaten for breakfast, they are much enjoyed at other meals and are often paired with cheese. A soufflé is quickly prepared for an attractive first course. An omelet, quiche or cheese tart makes a satisfying supper, accompanied by a green salad. People in rural areas traditionally ate what they produced on the farm – and eggs were always handy. Nowadays we may permit ourselves this simple yet rich fare less often, but eggs, along with cheese, are an essential part of the country kitchen.

CHEESE AND HAM CROISSANTS *Croissants au Fromage et Jambon*

These hot croissant "sandwiches" are an upscale version of croque monsieur, *classic café fare.*
They make a simple tasty lunch – try using different combinations of ham and cheese.

SERVES 2

2 large croissants
2 tbsp butter, softened
Dijon mustard
2 slices prosciutto
2–3 ounces Camembert or Brie (rind
*   removed), sliced ½ inch thick*
lettuce, tomatoes and chives, to serve

1 Preheat the oven to 400°F. Split
the croissants lengthwise and spread
each side with butter and a little
mustard.

2 ▼ Place a piece of ham on the
bottom half of each croissant,
trimming to fit. Place slices of
cheese on the ham and cover with
the croissant tops.

3 ▲ Place the croissants on a baking
sheet and cover them loosely with
foil, then bake for 3–5 minutes until
the cheese begins to melt. Serve with
lettuce, tomatoes and chives.

CHEESE PUFF RING *Gougère*

This light savory pastry comes from Burgundy, where it is traditionally served with red wine.

SERVES 6–8

¾ cup flour
¼ tsp salt
pinch of cayenne pepper
pinch of ground nutmeg
¾ cup water
6 tbsp butter, cut into pieces
3 eggs
3 ounces Swiss cheese, cut into ¼ inch
*   cubes*

1 Preheat the oven to 400°F.
Lightly grease a baking sheet. Sift
together the flour, salt, cayenne
pepper and nutmeg.

VARIATION

Stir in 1–2 tbsp chopped fresh
parsley or chives, or chopped
scallions before baking.

2 ▲ In a medium saucepan, bring
the water and butter to a boil.
Remove from the heat and add the
dry ingredients all at once. Beat with
a wooden spoon for about 1 minute
until the mixture is well blended and
starts to pull away from the sides of
the pan.

3 Place the pan over low heat and
cook for 2 minutes, beating
constantly, then remove the pan
from the heat.

4 Beat the eggs together in a small
bowl and then very gradually (one
tablespoon at a time), beat into the
mixture, beating thoroughly after
each addition until the dough is
smooth and shiny. It should pull
away and fall slowly when dropped
from a spoon – you may not need all
the beaten egg. Add the cubed
cheese and stir to mix well.

5 ▲ Using two large tablespoons,
drop adjoining mounds of dough
onto the baking sheet to form a
10 inch circle. Bake for 25–30
minutes until well browned. Cool
slightly on a wire rack and serve warm.

ALSATIAN LEEK AND ONION TARTLETS   *Tartlettes Alsaciennes*

The savory filling in these tartlets is traditional to northeastern France where many types of quiche are popular. Baking in individual pans makes for easier serving and looks attractive too.

SERVES 6

2 tbsp butter, cut into 8 pieces
l onion, thinly sliced
½ tsp dried thyme
1 pound leeks, thinly sliced
5 tbsp grated Swiss cheese
3 eggs
1¼ cups light cream
pinch of ground nutmeg
salt and freshly ground black pepper
lettuce and parsley leaves and cherry
     tomatoes, to serve
FOR THE PASTRY
1⅓ cup flour
6 tbsp cold butter
1 egg yolk
2–3 tbsp cold water
½ tsp salt

1 To make the pastry, sift the flour into a bowl and add the butter. Using your fingertips or a pastry blender, rub or cut the butter into the flour until the mixture resembles fine breadcrumbs.

2 ▲ Make a well in the flour mixture. In a small bowl, beat together the egg yolk, water and salt. Pour into the well and, using a fork, lightly combine the flour and liquid until the dough begins to stick together. Form into a flattened ball. Wrap and chill for 30 minutes.

3 ▲ Lightly butter six 4 inch tartlet pans. On a lightly floured surface, roll out the dough until about ⅛ inch thick, then using a 5 inch cutter, cut as many rounds as possible. Gently ease the pastry rounds into the pans, pressing the pastry firmly into the base and sides. Reroll the trimmings and line the remaining pans. Prick the bases and chill for 30 minutes.

4 ▲ Preheat the oven to 375°F. Line the pastry cases with foil and fill with baking beans. Place them on a baking sheet and bake for 6–8 minutes until the pastry edges are golden. Lift out the foil and beans and bake the pastry cases for 2 minutes more until the bases appear dry. Transfer to a wire rack to cool. Reduce temperature of the oven to 350°F.

5 ▲ In a large frying pan, melt the butter over medium heat, then add the onion and thyme and cook for 3–5 minutes until the onion is just softened, stirring frequently. Add the leeks and cook for 10–12 minutes until they are soft and tender. Divide the mixture among the pastry cases and sprinkle each with cheese, dividing it evenly.

6 ▲ In a medium bowl, beat together the eggs, cream, nutmeg and salt and pepper. Place the pastry cases on a baking sheet and pour in the egg mixture. Bake for 15–20 minutes until set and golden. Transfer the tartlets to a wire rack to cool slightly, then remove them from the pans and serve warm or at room temperature with lettuce and parsley leaves and cherry tomatoes.

TWICE-BAKED SOUFFLÉS

Soufflés Renversés

These little soufflés are served upside-down! They are remarkably easy to make and can be prepared up to a day in advance, then reheated in the sauce – perfect for easy entertaining.

SERVES 6

1½ tbsp butter
2 tbsp flour
⅔ cup milk
1 small bay leaf
ground nutmeg
2 eggs, separated, plus 1 egg white, at
    room temperature
⅔ cup grated Swiss cheese
¼ tsp cream of tartar
salt and freshly ground black pepper
FOR THE TOMATO CREAM SAUCE
1¼ cups heavy cream
2 tsp tomato purée
1 ripe tomato, peeled, seeded and
    finely diced
salt and cayenne pepper

1 Preheat the oven to 375°F. Generously butter six ¾ cup ramekins, then line the bases with buttered wax paper or non-stick baking paper. Set aside.

2 ▲ In a heavy saucepan over medium heat, melt the butter, stir in the flour and cook until just golden, stirring occasionally. Pour in about half the milk, whisking vigorously until smooth, then whisk in the remaining milk and add the bay leaf. Season with a little salt and plenty of pepper and nutmeg. Bring to a boil and cook, stirring constantly, for about 1 minute.

3 ▲ Remove the sauce from the heat and discard the bay leaf. Beat the egg yolks, one at a time, into the hot sauce, then stir in the cheese until it is melted. Set aside.

4 In a large, clean greasefree bowl, whisk the egg whites slowly until they become frothy. Add the cream of tartar, then increase the speed and whisk until they form peaks that just flop over at the top.

5 ▲ Stir a spoonful of beaten egg whites into the cheese sauce to lighten it. Pour the cheese sauce over the remaining whites. Using a rubber spatula or large metal spoon, gently fold the sauce into the whites.

COOK'S TIP

If making ahead, cool the cooked soufflés, then cover and chill. Bring the soufflés back to room temperature before reheating.

6 ▲ Spoon the soufflé mixture into the prepared dishes, filling them about three-quarters full. Put the dishes in a shallow baking dish and pour in boiling water to come halfway up the sides of the dishes. Bake for about 18 minutes until puffed and golden brown. Let the soufflés cool in the dishes long enough to deflate.

7 ▲ To make the sauce, bring the cream just to a boil in a small saucepan. Reduce the heat, stir in the tomato purée and diced tomato and cook for 2–3 minutes. Season with salt and cayenne pepper. Spoon a thin layer of sauce into a gratin dish just large enough to hold the soufflés. Run a knife around the edge of the soufflés and invert to unmold. Remove the lining paper if necessary. Pour the remaining sauce over the soufflés and bake for 12–15 minutes until well browned.

FISH
AND
SHELLFISH

The fervor for freshness and simplicity that characterizes French country cooking makes it perfect for fish and shellfish. With vast areas of coastline on two oceans, France has a superb array of seafood, changing with the seasons and the location, on offer in weekly markets in all its regions. Local fishermen sell the catch from the quayside or the beach all along the Mediterranean, where it is simmered in fish stews or simply baked or broiled. In Normandy and Brittany, mussels and scallops are gathered fresh from the sea and steamed or sautéed in butter. Uncomplicated country cooking highlights the fresh briny aromas and delicate flavors of almost all fish and shellfish.

SCALLOPS WITH MUSHROOMS   *Coquilles Saint Jacques au Gratin*

This dish has been a classic on bistro menus since Hemingway's days in Paris – it makes an appealing appetizer, or serve it as a rich and elegant main course.

SERVES 2–4

1 cup dry white wine
½ cup water
2 shallots, finely chopped
1 bay leaf
1 pound shelled scallops, rinsed
3 tbsp butter
3 tbsp flour
6 tbsp heavy cream
ground nutmeg
6 ounces mushrooms, thinly sliced
3–4 tbsp dry breadcrumbs
salt and freshly ground black pepper

1 ▼ Combine the wine, water, shallots and bay leaf in a medium saucepan. Bring to a boil, then reduce the heat to medium-low and simmer for 10 minutes. Add the scallops, cover and simmer for 3–4 minutes until they are opaque.

2 Remove the scallops from the cooking liquid with a slotted spoon and boil the liquid until reduced to ¾ cup. Strain the liquid.

3 ▲ Carefully pull off the tough muscle from the side of the scallops and discard. Slice the scallops in half crosswise.

4 ▲ Melt 2 tbsp of the butter in a heavy saucepan over medium-high heat. Stir in the flour and cook for 2 minutes. Add the reserved cooking liquid, whisking vigorously until smooth, then whisk in the cream and season with salt, pepper and nutmeg. Reduce the heat to low and simmer for 10 minutes, stirring frequently.

5 Melt the remaining butter in a frying pan over medium-high heat. Add the mushrooms and cook for about 5 minutes until lightly browned, stirring frequently. Stir the mushrooms into the sauce.

6 Preheat the broiler. Add the scallops to the sauce and adjust the seasoning. Spoon the mixture into four individual gratin dishes, large scallop shells or a flameproof baking dish and sprinkle with breadcrumbs. Broil until golden brown and bubbly.

MUSSELS STEAMED IN WHITE WINE   *Moules Marinières*

This is the best and easiest way to serve the small tender mussels, bouchots, *that are farmed along much of the French coast line. In Normandy the local sparkling dry cider is often used instead of white wine. Serve with plenty of crusty French bread to dip in the juices.*

<u>SERVES 4</u>

4½ pounds mussels
1¼ cups dry white wine
4–6 large shallots, finely chopped
bouquet garni
freshly ground black pepper

1 ▲ Discard any broken mussels and those with open shells that refuse to close when tapped. Under cold running water, scrape the mussel shells with a knife to remove any barnacles and pull out the stringy "beards." Soak the mussels in several changes of cold water for at least 1 hour.

2 ▲ In a large heavy flameproof casserole combine the wine, shallots, bouquet garni and plenty of pepper. Bring to a boil over medium-high heat and cook for 2 minutes.

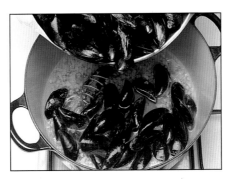

3 ▲ Add the mussels and cook, tightly covered, for 5 minutes, or until the mussels open, shaking and tossing the pan occasionally. Discard any mussels that do not open.

4 Using a slotted spoon, divide the mussels among warmed soup plates. Tilt the casserole a little and hold for a few seconds to allow any sand to settle to the bottom.

5 Spoon or pour the cooking liquid over the mussels, dividing it evenly, then serve at once.

VARIATION

For Mussels with Cream Sauce (*Moules à la Crème*), cook as above, but transfer the mussels to a warmed bowl and cover to keep warm. Strain the cooking liquid through a cheesecloth-lined colander into a large saucepan and boil for about 7–10 minutes to reduce by half. Stir in 6 tbsp heavy cream and 2 tbsp chopped parsley, then add the mussels. Cook for about 1 minute more to reheat the mussels.

MEDITERRANEAN FISH STEW

Bouillabaisse

Different variations of bouillabaisse *abound along the Mediterranean coast – every village seems to have its own version – and almost any combination of fish and shellfish can be used.*

SERVES 8

6 pounds white fish, such as sea bass, snapper or monkfish, filleted and skinned (choose thick fish)
3 tbsp extra virgin olive oil
grated rind of 1 orange
1 garlic clove, very finely chopped
pinch of saffron threads
2 tbsp Pernod (or other anise-flavored liqueur)
1 small fennel bulb, finely chopped
1 large onion, finely chopped
½ pound small new potatoes, sliced
2 pounds large raw Mediterranean shrimp, peeled
croûtons, to serve

FOR THE STOCK
2–3 pounds fish heads, bones and trimmings
2 tbsp olive oil
2 leeks, sliced
1 onion, halved and sliced
1 red bell pepper, cored and sliced
1½ pounds ripe tomatoes, cored and quartered
4 garlic cloves, sliced
bouquet garni
rind of ½ orange, removed with a vegetable peeler
2 or 3 pinches saffron threads

FOR THE ROUILLE
⅔ cup soft white breadcrumbs
1 or 2 garlic cloves, very finely chopped
½ red bell pepper, roasted
1 tsp tomato paste
½ cup extra virgin olive oil

COOK'S TIP

Be sure to ask the fish seller for the heads, tails and trimmings from your fish fillets and avoid strong-flavored oily fish, such as mackerel. To reduce last-minute work, you can make the *rouille*, croûtons and stock early in the day while the fish marinates.

1 ▲ Cut the fish fillets into serving pieces, then trim off any thin parts and reserve for the stock. Put the fish in a bowl with 2 tbsp of the olive oil, the orange rind, garlic, saffron and liqueur. Turn to coat well, cover and chill.

2 ▲ To make the stock, rinse the fish heads and bones under cold running water. Heat the olive oil in a large, preferably stainless steel, saucepan or flameproof casserole. Add the leeks, onion and pepper and cook over medium heat for about 5 minutes until the onion starts to soften, stirring occasionally. Add the fish heads, bones and trimmings, with any heads or shells from the shrimp. Then add the tomatoes, garlic, bouquet garni, orange rind, saffron and enough cold water to cover the ingredients by 1 inch.

3 Bring to a boil, skimming any foam that rises to the surface, then reduce the heat and simmer, covered, for ½ hour, skimming once or twice more. Strain the stock.

4 ▲ To make the *rouille*, soak the breadcrumbs in water then squeeze dry. Put the breadcrumbs in a food processor with the garlic, roasted red bell pepper and tomato paste and process until smooth. With the machine running, slowly pour the oil through the feed tube, scraping down the sides once or twice.

5 ▲ To finish the bouillabaise, heat the remaining 1 tbsp of olive oil in a wide flameproof casserole over a medium heat. Cook the fennel and onion for about 5 minutes until the onion just softens, then add the stock. Bring to a boil, add the potatoes and cook for 5–7 minutes. Reduce the heat to medium and add the fish, starting with the thickest pieces and adding the thinner ones after 2 or 3 minutes. Add the shrimp and continue simmering gently until all the fish and shellfish is cooked.

6 Transfer the fish, shellfish and potatoes to a heated tureen or soup plates. Adjust the seasoning and ladle the soup over. Serve with croûtons spread with *rouille*.

POTATO-TOPPED BAKED FISH

Poisson au Suquet

This informal fish bake is said to have originated with the fishermen on the Côte d'Azur who would cook the remains of their catch for lunch in the still-warm baker's oven.

SERVES 4

3 medium potatoes
2 onions, halved and sliced
2 tbsp olive oil, plus more for
    drizzling
2 garlic cloves, very finely chopped
1½ pounds thick skinless fish fillets,
    such as turbot or sea bass
1 bay leaf
1 thyme sprig
3 tomatoes, peeled and thinly sliced
2 tbsp orange juice
4 tbsp dry white wine
½ tsp saffron threads, steeped in 4 tbsp
    boiling water
salt and freshly ground black pepper

1 ▼ Cook the potatoes in boiling salted water for 15 minutes, then drain. When the potatoes are cool enough to handle, peel off the skins and slice them thinly.

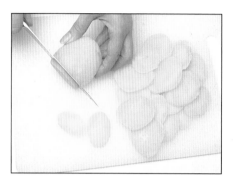

2 ▲ Meanwhile, in a heavy frying pan, fry the onions in the oil over medium-low heat for about 10 minutes, stirring frequently. Add the garlic and continue cooking for a few minutes until the onions are soft and golden.

3 Preheat the oven to 375°F. Layer half the potato slices in an 8 cup baking dish. Cover with half the onions. Season with salt and pepper.

4 ▲ Place the fish fillets on top of the vegetables and tuck in the herbs between them. Top with the tomato slices and then the remaining onions and potatoes.

5 Pour over the orange juice, wine and saffron liquid, season with salt and pepper and drizzle a little extra olive oil on top. Bake uncovered for about 30 minutes until the potatoes are tender and the fish is cooked.

COD WITH LENTILS AND LEEKS   *Morue aux Lentilles et Poireaux*

This unusual dish, discovered in a Parisian charcuterie, is great for entertaining. You can cook the vegetables ahead of time and let it bake while the first course is served.

SERVES 4

1 cup green lentils
1 bay leaf
1 garlic clove, finely chopped
grated rind of 1 orange
grated rind of 1 lemon
pinch of ground cumin
1 tbsp butter
1 pound leeks, thinly sliced or cut into
    julienne strips
1¼ cups heavy cream
1 tbsp lemon juice, or to taste
1¾ pounds thick skinless cod or
    haddock fillets
salt and freshly ground black pepper

1 Rinse the lentils and put them in a large saucepan with the bay leaf and garlic. Add enough water to cover by 2 inches. Bring to a boil, and boil gently for 10 minutes, then reduce the heat and simmer for 15–30 minutes more until the lentils are just tender.

2 ▲ Drain the lentils and discard the bay leaf, then stir in half the orange rind and all the lemon rind and season with ground cumin and salt and pepper. Transfer to a shallow baking dish or gratin dish. Preheat the oven to 375°F.

3 ▼ Melt the butter in a medium saucepan over medium heat, then add the leeks and cook, stirring frequently, until just softened. Add 1 cup of the cream and the remaining orange rind and cook gently for 15–20 minutes until the leeks are completely soft and the cream has thickened slightly. Stir in the lemon juice and season with salt and plenty of pepper.

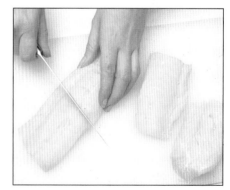

4 ▲ Cut the fish into four pieces, then, with your fingertips, locate and pull out any small bones. Season the fish with salt and pepper, place on top of the lentil mixture and press down slightly into the lentils. Cover each piece of fish with a quarter of the leek mixture and pour 1 tbsp of the remaining cream over each. Bake for about 30 minutes until the fish is cooked through and the topping is lightly golden.

SAUTÉED SCALLOPS   *Coquilles Saint Jacques Meunières*

Scallops go well with all sorts of sauces, but simple cooking is the best way to enjoy their flavor.

<u>SERVES 2</u>

1 pound shelled scallops
2 tbsp butter
2 tbsp dry white vermouth
1 tbsp finely chopped fresh parsley
salt and freshly ground black pepper

1 Rinse the scallops under cold running water to remove any sand or grit and pat dry using paper towels. Season them lightly with salt and pepper.

2 ▼ In a frying pan large enough to hold the scallops in one layer, heat half the butter until it begins to color. Sauté the scallops for 3–5 minutes, turning, until golden brown on both sides and just firm to the touch. Remove to a serving platter and cover to keep warm.

3 ▲ Add the vermouth to the hot frying pan, swirl in the remaining butter, add the parsley and pour the sauce over the scallops. Serve immediately.

GARLICKY SCALLOPS AND SHRIMP   *Fruits de Mer à la Provençale*

Scallops and shrimp are found all along the Atlantic and Mediterranean coasts of France and are enjoyed in every region. This method of cooking is typical in Provence.

<u>SERVES 2–4</u>

6 large sea scallops
6–8 large shrimp, peeled
flour, for dusting
2–3 tbsp olive oil
1 garlic clove, finely chopped
1 tbsp chopped fresh basil
2–3 tbsp lemon juice
salt and freshly ground black pepper

VARIATION

To make a richer sauce, transfer the cooked scallops and prawns to a warmed plate. Pour in 4 tbsp dry white wine and boil to reduce by half. Add 1 tbsp unsalted butter, whisking until it melts and the sauce thickens slightly. Pour over the scallops and shrimp.

---

1 ▼ Rinse the scallops under cold running water to remove any sand or grit. Pat them dry using paper towels and cut in half crosswise. Season the scallops and shrimp with salt and pepper and dust lightly with flour, shaking off the excess.

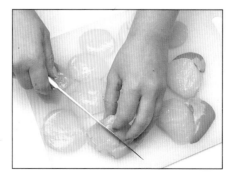

2 Heat the oil in a large frying pan over high heat and add the scallops and shrimp.

3 ▲ Reduce heat to medium-high and cook for 2 minutes, then turn the scallops and shrimp and add the garlic and basil, shaking pan to distribute them evenly. Cook for 2 minutes more until golden and just firm to the touch. Sprinkle over the lemon juice and toss to blend.

POULTRY AND GAME

Country cooking comes into its own with barnyard birds and woodland and water fowl. Poultry, especially chicken, is not only one of the most versatile foods, it is plentiful and relatively inexpensive, although that has not always been the case. At a country market, you can usually find a large selection of fresh, free-range chickens, ducks, guinea hens and game birds in season, perhaps still with their plumage. Hunting is a popular fall pastime in France and game, both wild and reared, is widely enjoyed. Favorite regional recipes, whether quickly sautéed with farm-fresh produce or long simmered for rich flavor, celebrate poultry and game.

CHICKEN WITH MORELS   *Suprêmes de Volaille Farcies aux Morilles*

Morels are among the most tasty dried mushrooms and, although expensive, a little goes a long way. Of course, you can use fresh morels (about 10 ounces) in place of the dried ones, or substitute chanterelles, shiitake or oyster mushrooms.

SERVES 4

1½ ounces dried morel mushrooms
1 cup chicken broth
4 tbsp butter
5 or 6 shallots, thinly sliced
3½ ounces button mushrooms, thinly
    sliced
¼ tsp dried thyme
2–3 tbsp brandy
¾ cup heavy cream
4 skinless boneless chicken breasts (about
    7 ounces each)
1 tbsp vegetable oil
¾ cup Champagne or dry sparkling
    wine
salt and freshly ground black pepper

1 ▲ Put the morels in a strainer and rinse well under cold running water, shaking to remove as much sand as possible. Put them in a saucepan with the broth and bring to a boil over medium-high heat. Remove the pan from the heat and leave to stand for 1 hour.

2 Remove the morels from the cooking liquid and strain the liquid through a cheesecloth-lined colander and reserve for the sauce. Reserve a few whole morels and slice the rest.

3 ▲ Melt half the butter in a frying pan over medium heat. Add the shallots and cook for 2 minutes until softened, then add the morels and mushrooms and cook, stirring frequently, for 2–3 minutes. Season and add the thyme, brandy and ⅓ cup of the cream. Reduce the heat and simmer gently for 10–12 minutes until any liquid has evaporated, stirring occasionally. Remove the morel mixture from the pan and set aside to cool slightly.

4 ▲ Pull off the finger-shaped piece on the underside from the chicken breasts and reserve for another use. Make a pocket in each chicken breast by cutting a slit along the thicker edge, taking care not to cut all the way through.

5 Using a small spoon, fill each pocket with one-quarter of the mushroom mixture, then if necessary, close with a toothpick.

6 ▲ Melt the remaining butter with the oil in a heavy frying pan over medium-high heat and cook the chicken breasts on one side for 6–8 minutes until golden. Transfer the chicken breasts to a plate. Add the Champagne or sparkling wine to the pan and boil to reduce by half. Add the strained morel cooking liquid and boil to reduce by half again.

7 ▲ Add the remaining cream and cook over medium heat for 2–3 minutes until the sauce thickens slightly and coats the back of a spoon. Adjust the seasoning. Return the chicken to the pan with any accumulated juices and the reserved whole morels and simmer for 3–5 minutes over medium-low heat until the chicken breasts are hot and the juices run clear when the meat is pierced with a knife.

OLD-FASHIONED CHICKEN FRICASSÉE *Fricassée de Poulet*

A fricassée *is a classic dish in which poultry or meat is first seared in fat, then braised with liquid until cooked. This recipe is finished with a little cream – leave it out if you wish.*

SERVES 4–6

2½–3 pounds chicken, cut into pieces
4 tbsp butter
2 tbsp vegetable oil
3 tbsp flour
1 cup dry white wine
3 cups chicken broth
bouquet garni
¼ tsp white pepper
8 ounces button mushrooms, trimmed
1 tsp lemon juice
16–24 small white onions, peeled
½ cup water
1 tsp sugar
6 tbsp heavy cream
salt
2 tbsp chopped fresh parsley,
    to garnish

1 ▲ Wash the chicken pieces, then pat dry with paper towels. Melt half the butter with the oil in a large, heavy flameproof casserole over medium heat. Add half the chicken pieces and cook for 10 minutes, turning occasionally, or until just golden in color. Transfer to a plate, then cook the remaining pieces in the same way.

COOK'S TIP

This dish can be made ahead and kept hot in a warm oven for up to an hour before serving.

2 ▲ Return the seared chicken pieces to the casserole. Sprinkle with the flour, turning the pieces to coat. Cook over low heat for about 4 minutes, turning occasionally.

3 ▲ Pour in the wine, bring to a boil and add the broth. Push the chicken pieces to one side and scrape the base of the casserole, stirring until well blended.

4 ▲ Bring the liquid to a boil, add the bouquet garni and season with a pinch of salt and white pepper. Cover and simmer over medium heat for 25–30 minutes until the chicken is tender and the juices run clear when the thickest part of the meat is pierced with a knife.

5 ▲ Meanwhile, in a frying pan, heat the remaining butter over medium-high heat. Add the mushrooms and lemon juice and cook for 3–4 minutes until the mushrooms are golden, stirring. Transfer the mushrooms to a bowl, add the onions, water and sugar to the pan, swirling to dissolve the sugar. Simmer for about 10 minutes, until just tender. Pour the onions and any juices into the bowl with the mushrooms and set aside.

6 When the chicken is cooked, transfer the pieces to a deep serving dish and cover with foil to keep warm. Discard the bouquet garni. Add any cooking juices from the vegetables to the casserole. Bring to a boil and boil, stirring frequently, until the sauce is reduced by half.

7 ▲ Whisk the cream into the sauce and cook for 2 minutes. Add the mushrooms and onions and cook for 2 minutes more. Adjust the seasoning, then pour the sauce over the chicken, sprinkle with parsley and serve.

CASSEROLED RABBIT WITH THYME *Fricassée de Lapin au Thym*

This is the sort of satisfying home cooking found in farmhouse kitchens and cozy neighbourhood restaurants in France, where rabbit is treated much like chicken and enjoyed frequently.

SERVES 4

2½ pounds rabbit
¼ cup flour
1 tbsp butter
1 tbsp olive oil
1 cup red wine
1½–2 cups chicken broth
1 tbsp fresh thyme leaves, or 2 tsp dried
    thyme
1 bay leaf
2 garlic cloves, finely chopped
2–3 tsp Dijon mustard
salt and freshly ground black pepper

1 Cut the rabbit into eight serving pieces: chop the saddle in half and separate the back legs into two pieces each; leave the front legs whole.

2 ▼ Put the flour in a plastic bag and season with salt and pepper. One at a time, drop the rabbit pieces into the bag and shake to coat them with flour. Tap off the excess, then discard any remaining flour.

3 ▲ Melt the butter with the oil over medium-high heat in a large flameproof casserole. Add the rabbit pieces and cook until golden, turning to color evenly.

4 ▲ Add the wine and boil for 1 minute then add enough of the broth just to cover the meat. Add the herbs and garlic, then simmer gently, covered, for 1 hour, or until the rabbit is very tender and the juices run clear when the thickest part of the meat is pierced with a knife.

5 ▲ Stir in the mustard, adjust the seasoning and strain the sauce. Arrange the rabbit pieces on a warmed serving platter with some sauce and serve the rest separately.

GUINEA HEN WITH CABBAGE

Pintade au Chou

Guinea hen is a domesticated relative of pheasant, so you can substitute pheasant or even chicken in this recipe. In some parts of France, such as Burgundy, garlic sausage may be added.

SERVES 4

2½–3 pound guinea hen
1 tbsp vegetable oil
1 tbsp butter
1 large onion, halved and sliced
1 large carrot, halved and sliced
1 large leek, sliced
1 pound green cabbage, such as savoy,
    sliced or chopped
½ cup dry white wine
½ cup chicken broth
1 or 2 garlic cloves, finely chopped
salt and freshly ground black pepper

1 Preheat the oven to 350°F. Tie the legs of the guinea hen with string.

2 ▲ Heat half the oil in a large flameproof casserole over medium-high heat and cook the guinea hen until golden brown on all sides. Transfer to a plate.

3 Pour out the fat from the casserole and add the remaining oil with the butter. Add the onion, carrot and leek and cook over low heat, stirring occasionally, for 5 minutes. Add the cabbage and cook for about 3–4 minutes until slightly wilted, stirring occasionally. Season the vegetables with salt and pepper.

4 ▼ Place the guinea hen on its side on the vegetables. Add the wine and bring to a boil, then add the broth and garlic. Cover and transfer to the oven. Cook for 25 minutes, then turn the bird onto the other side and cook for 20–25 minutes until it is tender and the juices run clear when the thickest part of the thigh is pierced with a knife.

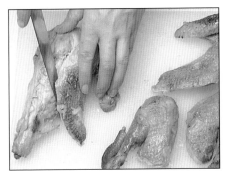

5 ▲ Transfer the bird to a board and let stand for 5–10 minutes, then cut into four or eight pieces. With a slotted spoon, transfer the cabbage to a warmed serving platter and place the guinea hen on top. Skim any fat from the cooking juices and serve separately.

ROAST PHEASANT WITH PORT
Faisan Rôti au Porto

Roasting the pheasant in foil keeps the flesh particularly moist. This recipe is best for very young birds and, if you have a choice, request the more tender female birds.

<u>SERVES 4</u>

2 oven-ready hen pheasants (about
   1½ pounds each)
4 tbsp unsalted butter, softened
8 fresh thyme sprigs
2 bay leaves
6 bacon slices
1 tbsp flour
¾ cup game or chicken broth, plus more
   if needed
1 tbsp red currant jelly
3–4 tbsp port
freshly ground black pepper

1 Preheat the oven to 450°F. Line a large roasting pan with a sheet of strong foil large enough to enclose the pheasants. Lightly brush the foil with oil.

2 ▼ Wipe the pheasants with damp paper towels and remove any extra fat or skin. Using your fingertips, carefully loosen the skin of the breasts. With a round-bladed knife or small spatula, spread the butter between the skin and breast meat of each bird. Tie the legs securely with string then lay the thyme sprigs and a bay leaf over the breast of each bird.

3 ▲ Lay bacon slices over the breasts, place the birds in the foil-lined pan and season with pepper. Bring together the long ends of the foil, fold over securely to enclose, then seal the ends.

4 Roast the birds for 20 minutes, then reduce the oven temperature to 375°F and cook for 40 minutes more. Uncover the birds and roast 10–15 minutes more or until they are browned and the juices run clear when the thigh of a bird is pierced with a knife. Transfer the birds to a board and let stand, covered with clean foil, for 10 minutes before carving.

5 ▲ Pour the juices from the foil into the roasting pan and skim off any fat. Sprinkle in the flour and cook over medium heat, stirring until smooth. Whisk in the broth and red currant jelly and bring to a boil. Simmer until the sauce thickens slightly, adding more broth if needed, then stir in the port and adjust the seasoning. Strain and serve with the pheasant.

DUCK STEW WITH OLIVES

Ragoût de Canard aux Olives

This method of preparing duck has its roots in Provence. The sweetness of the onions, which are not typical in all regional versions, balances the saltiness of the olives.

SERVES 6–8

2 ducks (about 3¼ pounds each),
    quartered, or 8 duck leg quarters
½ pound pearl onions
2 tbsp flour
1½ cups dry red wine
2 cups duck or chicken broth
bouquet garni
1 cup pitted green or black olives, or a
    combination
salt, if needed, and freshly ground black
    pepper

1 Put the duck pieces, skin side down, in a large frying pan over medium heat and cook for 10–12 minutes until well browned, turning to color evenly and cooking in batches if necessary. Pour off the fat from the pan.

2 Heat 1 tbsp of the duck fat in a large flameproof casserole and cook the onions, covered, over medium-low heat until evenly browned, stirring frequently. Sprinkle with flour and continue cooking, uncovered, for 2 minutes, stirring frequently.

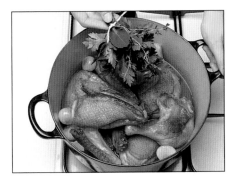

3 ▲ Stir in the wine and bring to a boil, then add the duck pieces, broth and bouquet garni. Bring to a boil, then reduce the heat to very low and simmer, covered, for about 40 minutes, stirring occasionally.

4 ▼ Rinse the olives in several changes of cold water. If they are very salty, put in a saucepan, cover with water and bring to a boil, then drain and rinse. Add the olives to the casserole and continue cooking for 20 minutes more until the duck is very tender.

5 Transfer the duck pieces, onions and olives to a plate. Strain the cooking liquid, skim off all the fat and return the liquid to the pan. Boil to reduce by about one-third, then adjust the seasoning and return the duck and vegetables to the casserole. Simmer gently for a few minutes to heat through.

COOK'S TIP

If you take the breasts from whole ducks for duck breast recipes, freeze the legs until you have enough for this stew, and make stock from the carcasses.

61

MEAT DISHES

Meat is a mainstay of French country cooking. A pot of stew simmering on the back of the stove fills the farmhouse kitchen with enticing aromas and makes life easy for the cook. The pig from a neighboring farm provides ham, sausages and succulent pork throughout the year. Sometimes these meats are combined with beans, lentils or sauerkraut for a hearty and warming treat. And what would Sunday lunch be without a roast – perhaps lamb served with vegetables from the garden. Every region has its traditional specialties for savory meat dishes and even in coastal areas the main course of the rural midday meal is likely to be meat.

BURGUNDY BEEF STEW

Boeuf Bourguignon

Tradition dictates that you should use the same wine in this stew that you plan to serve with it, but a less expensive full-bodied wine will do for cooking. The stew reheats very well.

SERVES 6

3½ pounds lean stewing beef (chuck or shin)
6 ounces lean salt pork or thick cut bacon
3 tbsp butter
¾ pound pearl onions
¾ pound small button mushrooms
1 onion, finely chopped
1 carrot, finely chopped
2 or 3 garlic cloves, finely chopped
3 tbsp flour
3 cups red wine, preferably Burgundy
1½ tbsp tomato paste
bouquet garni
2½–3 cups beef broth
1 tbsp chopped fresh parsley
salt and freshly ground black pepper

1 ▲ Cut the beef into 2 inch pieces and dice the salt pork or cut the bacon crosswise into thin strips.

2 In a large heavy flameproof casserole, cook the pork or bacon over medium heat until golden brown, then remove with a slotted spoon and drain. Pour off all but 2 tbsp of the fat.

3 ▲ Increase the heat to medium-high. Add enough meat to the pan to fit easily in one layer (do not crowd the pan or the meat will not brown) and cook, turning to color all sides, until well browned. Transfer the beef to a plate and continue browning the meat in batches.

4 ▲ In a heavy frying pan, melt one-third of the butter over medium heat, add the pearl onions and cook, stirring frequently, until evenly golden. Set aside on a plate.

5 ▲ In the same pan, melt half of the remaining butter over medium heat. Add the mushrooms and sauté, stirring frequently, until golden, then set aside with the pearl onions.

6 ▲ When all the beef has been browned, pour off any fat from the casserole and add the remaining butter. When the butter has melted, add the onion, carrot and garlic and cook over medium heat for 3–4 minutes until just softened, stirring frequently. Sprinkle over the flour and cook for 2 minutes, then add the wine, tomato paste and bouquet garni. Bring to a boil, scraping the base of the pan.

7 ▲ Return the beef and bacon to the casserole and pour on the broth, adding more if needed to cover the meat and vegetables when pressed down. Cover the casserole and simmer very gently over low heat, stirring occasionally, for about 3 hours or until the meat is very tender. Add the sautéed mushrooms and pearl onions and cook, covered, for 30 minutes more. Discard the bouquet garni and stir in the parsley before serving.

STEAK WITH ANCHOVY SAUCE *Entrecôte au Beurre d'Anchois*

This may sound like an unusual combination, but the anchovy adds flavor without tasting fishy.

SERVES 2

3 tbsp butter
4 shallots, finely chopped
1 garlic clove, crushed
6 tbsp heavy cream
1½ tbsp anchovy paste
1 tbsp chopped fresh tarragon
2 sirloin or fillet steaks, about
7–9 ounces each
2 tsp vegetable oil
salt and freshly ground black pepper
parsley or tarragon sprigs, to garnish
sautéed potatoes, to serve

1 ▼ Melt 2 tbsp of the butter in a small saucepan and sauté the shallots and garlic until they are just soft. Stir in the cream, anchovy paste and tarragon, and simmer very gently for about 10 minutes.

2 ▲ Season the steaks. Heat the remaining butter with the oil in a heavy frying pan over medium-high heat until it begins to brown.

3 Add the meat and cook for about 6–8 minutes, turning once, until done as preferred (medium-rare meat will still be slightly soft when pressed, medium meat will be springy and well-done firm). Transfer the steaks to warmed serving plates and cover to keep warm.

4 ▲ Add 2 tbsp of water to the frying pan. Stir in the anchovy sauce and cook for 1–2 minutes, stirring and scraping the bottom of the pan. Adjust the seasoning and pour the sauce over the meat, then garnish with parsley or tarragon and serve with potatoes.

VARIATION

To make a tomato cream sauce to serve with the steak, substitute 1–2 tsp tomato paste for the anchovy paste.

VEAL KIDNEYS WITH MUSTARD   *Rognons de Veau à la Moutarde*

In France, veal kidneys are easily found, but this dish is equally delicious made with lambs' kidneys. Be sure not to cook the sauce too long once the mustard is added or it will lose its piquancy.

SERVES 4

2 veal kidneys or 8–10 lamb kidneys,
    trimmed and membranes removed
2 tbsp butter
1 tbsp vegetable oil
4 ounces button mushrooms, quartered
4 tbsp chicken broth
2 tbsp brandy (optional)
¾ cup crème fraîche or heavy cream
2 tbsp Dijon mustard
salt and freshly ground black pepper
snipped fresh chives, to garnish

1 ▲ Cut the veal kidneys into pieces, discarding any fat. If using lambs' kidneys, remove the central core by cutting a V-shape from the middle of each kidney. Cut each kidney into three or four pieces.

2 ▲ In a large frying pan, melt the butter with the oil over high heat and swirl to blend. Add the kidneys and sauté for about 3–4 minutes, stirring frequently, until well browned, then transfer them to a plate using a slotted spoon.

3 ▲ Add the mushrooms to the pan and sauté for 2–3 minutes until golden, stirring frequently. Pour in the chicken broth and brandy, if using, then bring to a boil and boil for 2 minutes.

4 ▼ Stir in the crème fraîche or heavy cream and cook for about 2–3 minutes until the sauce is slightly thickened. Stir in the mustard and season with salt and pepper, then add the kidneys and cook for 1 minute to reheat. Scatter over the chives before serving.

ROAST STUFFED LAMB

Gigot Farci

The lambs that graze in the salty marshes along the north coast of Brittany and Normandy are considered the best in France. The stuffing is suitable for either leg or shoulder joints.

SERVES 6–8

*4–4½ pound boneless leg or shoulder of
  lamb (not tied)*
2 tbsp butter, softened
1–2 tbsp flour
½ cup white wine
1 cup chicken or beef broth
salt and freshly ground black pepper
watercress, to garnish
sautéed potatoes, to serve
FOR THE STUFFING
5 tbsp butter
1 small onion, finely chopped
1 garlic clove, finely chopped
⅓ cup long grain rice
⅔ cup chicken broth
½ tsp dried thyme
4 lamb kidneys, halved and cored
*10 ounces young spinach leaves,
  well washed*
salt and freshly ground black pepper

1 ▲ To make the stuffing, melt 2 tbsp of the butter in a saucepan over medium heat. Add the onion' and cook for 2–3 minutes until just softened, then add the garlic and rice and cook for about 1–2 minutes until the rice appears translucent, stirring constantly. Add the broth, salt and pepper and thyme and bring to a boil, stirring occasionally, then reduce the heat to low and cook for about 18 minutes, covered, until the rice is tender and the liquid is absorbed. Spoon the rice into a bowl and fluff with a fork.

2 In a small frying pan, melt about 2 tbsp of the remaining butter over medium-high heat. Add the kidneys and cook for about 2–3 minutes, turning once, until lightly browned, but still pink inside, then transfer to a board and let cool. Cut the kidneys into pieces and add to the rice, season with salt and pepper and toss to combine.

3 ▲ In a frying pan, heat the remaining butter over medium heat until foaming. Add the spinach leaves and cook for 1–2 minutes until wilted, drain off excess liquid, then transfer the spinach to a plate and let cool.

4 ▲ Preheat the oven to 375°F. Lay the meat skin-side down on a work surface and season with salt and pepper. Spread the spinach leaves in an even layer over the surface then spread the stuffing in an even layer over the spinach. Roll up the meat like a jelly roll and use a skewer to close the seam.

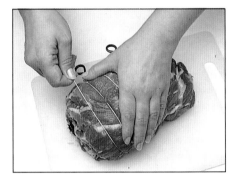

5 ▲ Tie the meat at 1 inch intervals to hold its shape, then place in a roasting pan, spread with the softened butter and season with salt and pepper. Roast for 1½–2 hours until the juices run slightly pink when pierced with a skewer, or until a meat thermometer inserted into the thickest part of the meat registers 135–140°F for medium-rare to medium. Transfer the meat to a carving board, cover loosely with foil and let rest for about 20 minutes.

6 Skim off as much fat from the roasting pan as possible, then place the pan over medium-high heat and bring to a boil. Sprinkle over the flour and cook for 2–3 minutes until browned, stirring and scraping the base of the pan. Whisk in the wine and broth and bring to a boil, then cook for 4–5 minutes until the sauce thickens. Season and strain into a gravy boat. Carve the meat into slices, garnish with watercress and serve with the gravy and potatoes.

VARIATION

If kidneys are difficult to obtain, substitute about ¼ pound mushrooms. Chop coarsely and cook in butter until tender. Don't use dark mushrooms – they will make the rice a murky color.

Sauerkraut with Pork and Sausages *Choucroûte Garnie*

This Alsatian specialty shows the German influence on the region's cuisine. Strasbourg is renowned for its pork and beef sausages – use them if you can.

Serves 8

2 tbsp vegetable oil
1 onion, halved and sliced
4 ounces smoked bacon slices, chopped
2 pounds bottled sauerkraut, well rinsed
    and drained
1 apple, peeled and sliced
1 or 2 bay leaves
½ tsp dried thyme
4–5 juniper berries
1 cup dry white wine
½ cup apple juice or water
6 Strasbourg sausages, knackwurst or
    frankfurters
6 spareribs
2 pounds small potatoes, peeled
4 pork chops or ham steaks
salt and freshly ground black pepper

1 ▼ Preheat the oven to 300°F. Heat half the oil in a large flameproof casserole over medium heat, then add the sliced onion and chopped bacon and cook, stirring occasionally for about 5 minutes until the onion is soft and the bacon just colored.

2 ▲ Tilt the pan, spoon off the fat, then stir in the sauerkraut, apple, bay leaves, thyme, juniper berries, wine and apple juice or water. Cover the casserole, place in the oven and cook for 30 minutes.

3 In a second large flameproof casserole, heat the remaining oil over medium-high heat and add the spareribs. Cook, turning frequently, until browned on all sides. Add the spareribs to the other casserole with the sausages and cook, covered, for 1½ hours, stirring occasionally.

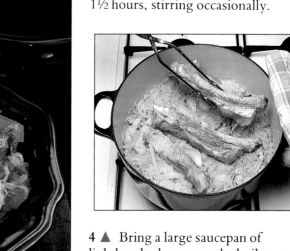

4 ▲ Bring a large saucepan of lightly salted water to the boil over medium-high heat. Add the potatoes and cook for 10 minutes. Drain and add to the casserole with the pork chops. Push them into the sauerkraut and continue cooking, covered, for 30–45 minutes more. Season with salt, if needed, and pepper before serving.

TOULOUSE CASSOULET   *Cassoulet*

There are as many versions of this regional specialty in Southwest France as there are towns.

SERVES 6–8

1 pound dried white beans (navy or
*   cannellini), soaked overnight in cold*
*   water, then rinsed and drained*
1½ pounds French garlic sausages
1¼ pounds each boneless lamb and pork
*   shoulder, cut into 2 inch pieces*
1 large onion, finely chopped
3 or 4 garlic cloves, very finely chopped
4 tomatoes, peeled, seeded and chopped
1¼ cups chicken broth
bouquet garni
4 tbsp fresh bread crumbs
salt and freshly ground black pepper

1 Put the beans in a saucepan with water to cover. Boil vigorously for 10 minutes and drain, then return to a clean saucepan, cover with water and bring to a boil. Reduce the heat and simmer for 45 minutes, or until tender, then add a little salt and let soak in the cooking water.

2 ▲ Preheat the oven to 350°F. Prick the sausages, place them in a large heavy frying pan over medium heat and cook for 20–25 minutes until browned, turning occasionally. Drain on paper towels and pour off all but 1 tbsp of the fat from the pan.

3 Increase the heat to medium-high. Season the lamb and pork and add enough of the meat to the pan to fit easily in one layer. Cook until browned, then transfer to a large dish. Continue browning in batches.

4 Add the onion and garlic to the pan and cook for 3–4 minutes until just soft, stirring. Stir in the tomatoes and cook for 2–3 minutes, then transfer the vegetables to the meat dish. Add the broth and bring to a boil, then skim off the fat.

5 ▲ Spoon a quarter of the beans into a large casserole, and top with a third of the sausages, meat and vegetables.

6 Continue layering, ending with a layer of beans. Tuck in the bouquet garni, pour over the broth and top up with enough of the bean cooking liquid to just cover.

7 Cover the casserole and bake for 2 hours (check and add more bean cooking liquid if it seems dry). Uncover the casserole, sprinkle over the bread crumbs and press with the back of a spoon to moisten them. Continue cooking the cassoulet, uncovered, for about 20 minutes more until browned.

COUNTRY-STYLE PÂTÉ WITH LEEKS   *Pâté de Porc aux Poireaux*

Traditionally this sort of pork pâté (or more correctly, terrine, since it has no crust) contains pork liver and egg to bind. This version uses leeks instead for a fresher flavor and a lighter result.

SERVES 8–10

1 pound trimmed leeks (white and light
    green parts)
1 tbsp butter
2 or 3 large garlic cloves, finely chopped
2¼ pounds lean pork leg or shoulder
5 ounces smoked bacon strips
1½ tsp chopped fresh thyme
3 sage leaves, finely chopped
¼ tsp quatre èpices (a mix of ground
    cloves, cinnamon, nutmeg and
    pepper)
¼ tsp ground cumin
pinch of freshly grated nutmeg
½ tsp salt
1 tsp freshly ground black pepper
1 bay leaf

1 ▲ Cut the leeks lengthwise, wash well and slice thinly. Melt the butter in a large heavy saucepan, add the leeks, then cover and cook over medium-low heat for 10 minutes, stirring occasionally. Add the garlic and continue cooking for about 10 minutes until the leeks are very soft, then set aside to cool.

COOK'S TIP

In France, *cornichons* (small dill pickles) and mustard are traditional accompaniments for pork terrines along with slices of crusty baguette.

2 ▲ Trim all the fat, tendons and connective tissue from the pork and cut the meat into 1¾ inch cubes. Working in two or three batches, put the meat into a food processor fitted with the metal blade; the bowl should be about half-full. Pulse to chop the meat to a coarse purée. Alternatively, pass the meat through the coarse blade of a meat grinder. Transfer the meat to a large mixing bowl and remove any white stringy pieces.

3 Reserve two of the bacon strips for garnishing, and chop or grind the remaining bacon strips. Add the chopped or ground bacon to the pork in the bowl.

4 Preheat the oven to 350°F. Line the base and sides of a 6¼ cup terrine or loaf pan with wax paper or non-stick baking paper.

5 ▲ Add the leeks, herbs, spices and salt and pepper to the bowl with the pork and bacon and, using a wooden spoon or your fingertips, mix until well combined.

6 ▲ Spoon the mixture into the terrine or loaf pan, pressing it into the corners and compacting it. Tap firmly to settle the mixture and smooth the top. Arrange the bay leaf and bacon strips on top, then cover tightly with foil.

7 ▲ Place the terrine or loaf pan in a roasting pan and pour boiling water to come halfway up the sides. Bake for 1¼ hours.

8 Lift the terrine out of the roasting pan and pour out the water. Put the terrine back in the pan and place a baking sheet or board on top. If the pâté has not risen above the sides of the terrine, place a foil-covered board inside the pan to lie directly on the pâté. Weight with two or three large cans or other heavy objects while it cools. (Liquid will seep out which is why the terrine should stand inside a roasting pan.) Chill until cold, preferably overnight, before slicing.

PASTRY AND CAKES

Home baking is a recent development in rural areas of France, where the communal bread oven was used for baking cakes and tarts in the heat remaining from the weekly batch of bread. Now *pâtisseries* appear in practically every town and a country market usually has a stall of regional sweets, such as the traditional butter cookies of Brittany. Elaborate pastries and cakes are normally the province of professionals, but country cooks are more likely than their urban counterparts to make tea cakes and fruit tarts themselves – apple tarts are a great way to use windfall apples from the orchard – and most have a treasured recipe for a rich, homey chocolate cake.

POUND CAKE WITH RED FRUIT   *Quatre Quarts aux Fruits*

Quatre quarts literally translates as "four quarters," in this case, the equal weights of the four main ingredients. This orange-scented cake is good for tea or as a dessert with a fruit coulis.

<u>SERVES 6–8</u>

1 pound fresh raspberries, strawberries or
   pitted cherries, or a combination of
   any of these
⅞ cup superfine sugar, plus
   1–2 tbsp and some for sprinkling
1 tbsp lemon juice
1⅓ cups flour
2 tsp baking powder
pinch of salt
¾ cup unsalted butter, softened
3 eggs, at room temperature
grated zest of 1 orange
1 tbsp orange juice

1 Reserve a few whole fruits for decorating. In a food processor fitted with the metal blade, process the fruit until smooth.

2 ▼ Add 1–2 tbsp of the sugar and the lemon juice to the fruit purée, then process again to blend. Strain the sauce and chill.

3 Butter the base and sides of an 8×4 inch loaf pan or an 8 inch springform pan and line the base with nonstick baking paper. Butter the paper and the sides of the pan again, then sprinkle lightly with sugar and tap out any excess from the pan. Preheat the oven to 350°F.

4 ▲ Sift the flour, baking powder and a pinch of salt. In a medium bowl, beat the butter with an electric mixer for 1 minute until creamy. Add the sugar and beat for 4–5 minutes until very light and fluffy, then add the eggs, one at a time, beating well after each addition. Beat in the orange zest and juice.

5 ▲ Gently fold the flour mixture into the butter mixture in three batches, then spoon the mixture into the prepared pan and tap gently to release any air bubbles.

6 Bake the cake for 35–40 minutes until the top is golden and springs back when touched. Transfer the cake in its pan to a wire rack and leave to cool for 10 minutes. Remove the cake from the pan, then cool for about ½ hour. Remove the paper and serve slices or wedges of the warm cake with a little of the fruit sauce and decorate with the reserved fruit.

INDIVIDUAL BRIOCHES   *Petites Brioches*

These buttery rolls with their distinctive little topknots are delicious with a spoonful or two of jam and a cup of café au lait – or try them split and filled with scrambled eggs.

<u>MAKES 8</u>

scant 1 tbsp active dry yeast
1 tbsp superfine sugar
2 tbsp warm milk
2 eggs
1½ cups flour
½ tsp salt
6 tbsp butter, cut into 6 pieces, at room temperature
1 egg yolk beaten with 2 tsp water, for glazing

1 ▲ Lightly butter eight individual brioche pans or muffin cups. Put the yeast and sugar in a small bowl, add the milk and stir until dissolved. Let stand for about 5 minutes until foamy, then beat in the egg.

2 ▲ Put the flour and salt into a food processor fitted with the metal blade, then with the machine running, slowly pour in the yeast mixture. Scrape down the sides and continue processing for about 2–3 minutes, or until the dough forms a ball. Add the butter and pulse about 10 times, or until the butter is incorporated.

3 Transfer the dough to a lightly buttered bowl and cover with a cloth. Set aside to rise in a warm place for about 1 hour until doubled in size, then punch down.

4 ▲ Set aside quarter of the dough. Shape the remaining dough into eight balls and put into the prepared pans. Shape the reserved dough into eight smaller balls, then make a depression in the top of each large ball and set a small ball into it.

5 Allow the brioches to rise in a warm place for about 30 minutes until doubled in size. Preheat the oven to 400°F.

6 Brush the brioches lightly with the egg glaze and bake them for 15–18 minutes until golden brown. Transfer to a wire rack and let cool before serving.

COOK'S TIP

The dough may also be baked in the characteristic large brioche pan with sloping fluted sides. Put about three-quarters of the dough into the pan and set the remainder in a depression in the top, cover and let rise for about 1 hour, then bake for 35–45 minutes.

BRITTANY BUTTER COOKIES

Petites Gâteaux Bretons

These little cookies are similar to shortbread, but richer. Like most of the cakes and pastries from this province, they are made with the lightly salted butter, beurre demi-sel, from around Nantes.

MAKES 18–20

6 egg yolks, lightly beaten
1 tbsp milk
2 cups flour
⅞ cup superfine sugar
⅞ cup lightly salted butter, at room
   temperature, cut into small pieces

COOK'S TIP

To make one large Brittany Butter Cake, pat the dough with well floured hands into a 9 inch loose-based cake pan or springform pan. Brush with egg glaze and score the lattice pattern on top. Bake for 45 minutes–1 hour until firm to the touch and golden brown.

---

1 Preheat the oven to 350°F. Lightly butter a large heavy baking sheet. Mix 1 tbsp of the egg yolks with the milk to make a glaze and set aside.

2 ▲ Sift the flour into a large bowl and make a well in the center. Add the egg yolks, sugar and butter and, using your fingertips, work them together until smooth and creamy.

3 ▲ Gradually add a little flour at a time from the edge of the well, working it to form a smooth and slightly sticky dough.

4 ▲ Using floured hands, pat out the dough to about ½ inch thick and cut out rounds using a 3 inch cookie cutter. Transfer the rounds to a baking sheet, brush each with a little egg glaze, then using the back of a knife, score with lines to create a lattice pattern.

5 Bake the cookies for about 12–15 minutes until golden. Cool in the pan on a wire rack for 15 minutes, then carefully remove the cookies and let cool completely on the rack. Store in an airtight container.

SPICED-NUT PALMIERS

Palmiers

These delicate pastries, said to resemble palm trees, are popular throughout France. They are often simply rolled in sugar, but in this recipe the filling includes cinnamon and nuts.

MAKES ABOUT 40

½ cup chopped almonds, walnuts or
    hazelnuts
2 tbsp superfine sugar, plus some for
    sprinkling
½ tsp ground cinnamon
½ pound puff pastry, defrosted
    if frozen
1 egg, lightly beaten

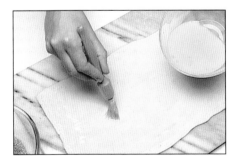

1 ▲ Lightly butter two large baking sheets, preferably non-stick. In a food processor fitted with the metal blade, process the nuts, sugar and cinnamon until finely ground. Transfer half to a small bowl.

2 ▲ Sprinkle the work surface and pastry with sugar and roll out the pastry to a 20×8 inch rectangle about ⅛ inch thick, sprinkling with more sugar as necessary. Brush the pastry lightly with beaten egg and sprinkle evenly with half of the nut mixture in the bowl.

3 ▼ Fold in the long edges of the pastry to meet in the center and flatten with the rolling pin. Brush with egg and sprinkle with most of the nut mixture. Fold in the edges again to meet in the center, brush with egg and sprinkle with the remaining nut mixture. Fold one side of the pastry over the other.

4 Using a sharp knife, cut the pastry crosswise into ⅜ inch thick slices and place the pieces cut-side down about 1 inch apart on the prepared baking sheets.

5 ▲ Spread the pastry edges apart to form a wedge shape. Chill the palmiers for at least 15 minutes. Preheat oven to 425°F.

6 Bake the palmiers for about 8–10 minutes until golden, carefully turning them over halfway through the cooking time. Watch carefully as the sugar can easily scorch. Transfer to a wire rack to cool.

79

LEMON TART

Tarte au Citron

This tart has a refreshing tangy flavor. You can find it in bistros and pâtisseries all over France.

<u>SERVES 8–10</u>

12 ounces shortcrust or sweet shortcrust
   pastry
grated rind of 2 or 3 lemons
⅔ cup freshly squeezed lemon juice
½ cup superfine sugar
4 tbsp crème fraîche or heavy cream
4 eggs, plus 3 egg yolks
confectioner's sugar, for dusting

1 ▼ Preheat the oven to 375°F. Roll out the pastry thinly and use to line a 9 inch pie pan. Prick the base of the pastry.

2 ▲ Line the pastry shell with foil and fill with baking beans. Bake for about 15 minutes until the edges are set and dry. Remove the foil and beans and continue baking for 5–7 minutes more until golden.

3 ▲ Place the lemon rind, juice and sugar in a bowl. Beat until combined and then gradually add the crème fraîche or heavy cream and beat until well blended.

4 ▲ Beat in the eggs, one at a time, then beat in the egg yolks and pour the filling into the pastry shell. Bake for 15–20 minutes, until the filling is set. If the pastry begins to brown too much, cover the edges with foil. Let cool. Dust with confectioner's sugar before serving.

FRENCH CHOCOLATE CAKE

Gâteau au Chocolat

This is typical of a French homemade cake – dense, dark and delicious. The texture is very different from a sponge cake and it is excellent served with cream or a fruit coulis.

SERVES 10–12

¾ cup superfine sugar, plus some for
   sprinkling
10 ounces semisweet chocolate,
   chopped
¾ cup unsalted butter, cut into
   pieces
2 tsp vanilla extract
5 eggs, separated
¼ cup flour, sifted
pinch of salt
confectioner's sugar, for dusting

1 ▲ Preheat the oven to 325°F. Generously butter a 9½ inch springform pan, then sprinkle the pan with a little sugar and tap out the excess.

2 Set aside 3 tbsp of the sugar. Place the chocolate, butter and remaining sugar in a heavy saucepan and cook over low heat until the chocolate and butter have melted and the sugar has dissolved. Remove the pan from the heat, stir in the vanilla extract and let the mixture cool slightly.

3 ▼ Beat the egg yolks into the chocolate mixture, beating each in well, then stir in the flour.

4 In a clean greasefree bowl, using an electric mixer, beat the egg whites slowly until they are frothy. Increase the speed, add the salt and continue beating until soft peaks form. Sprinkle over the reserved sugar and beat until the whites are stiff and glossy. Beat one-third of the whites into the chocolate mixture, then fold in the remaining whites.

5 ▲ Carefully pour the mixture into the pan and tap the pan gently to release any air bubbles.

6 Bake the cake for about 35–45 minutes until well risen and the top springs back when touched lightly with a fingertip. (If the cake appears to rise unevenly, rotate after 20–25 minutes.) Transfer the cake to a wire rack, remove the side of the pan and let cool completely. Remove the pan base. Dust the cake with confectioner's sugar and transfer to a serving plate.

APPLE TART

Tarte aux Pommes

This easy-to-make apple tart has rustic charm – it is just as you might find in a French farmhouse. Cooking the apples before putting them on the pastry prevents a soggy crust.

SERVES 6

2 pounds medium cooking apples, peeled, quartered and cored
1 tbsp lemon juice
¼ cup superfine sugar
4 tbsp butter
¾ pound shortcrust or sweet pastry (pâte sucrée)
crème fraîche or lightly whipped cream, to serve

VARIATION

For Spiced Pear Tart, substitute pears for the apples, cooking them for about 10 minutes until golden. Sprinkle with ½ tsp ground cinnamon and a pinch of ground cloves and stir to combine before arranging on the pastry.

1 Cut each cooking apple quarter lengthwise into two or three slices. Sprinkle with lemon juice and sugar and toss to combine.

2 ▲ Melt the butter in a large heavy frying pan over medium heat and add the apples. Cook, stirring frequently, for about 12 minutes until the apples are just golden brown. Remove the frying pan from the heat and set aside. Preheat the oven to 375°F.

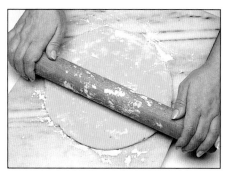

3 ▲ On a lightly floured surface, roll out the pastry to a 12 inch round and trim the edge if uneven. Carefully transfer the pastry round to a baking sheet.

4 ▲ Spoon the apple slices onto the pastry round, heaping them up, and leaving a 2 inch border all around the edge of the pastry.

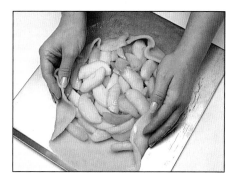

5 ▲ Turn up the pastry border and gather it around the apples to enclose the outside apples. Bake the tart for 35–40 minutes until the pastry is crisp and browned. Serve warm, with crème fraîche or cream.

PEAR AND ALMOND CREAM TART   *Tarte aux Poires Frangipane*

This tart is equally successful made with other kinds of fruit, and some variation can be seen in almost every good French pâtisserie. Try making it with nectarines, peaches, apricots or apples.

SERVES 6

3 firm pears
lemon juice
¾ pound shortcrust or sweet shortcrust pastry
1 tbsp peach brandy or water
4 tbsp peach jam, strained
FOR THE ALMOND CREAM FILLING
¾ cup blanched whole almonds
¼ cup superfine sugar
5 tbsp butter
1 egg, plus 1 egg white
few drops almond extract

1 ▲ Roll out pastry thinly and use to line a 9 inch pie pan. Chill the pastry case while you make the filling. Put the almonds and sugar in a food processor fitted with the metal blade and pulse until finely ground; they should not be pasty. Add the butter and process until creamy, then add the egg, egg white and almond extract and mix well.

2 Place a baking sheet in the oven and preheat to 375°F. Peel the pears, halve them, remove the cores and rub with lemon juice. Put the pear halves cut side down on a board and slice thinly crosswise, keeping the slices together.

3 ▲ Pour the almond cream filling into the pastry shell. Slide a spatula under one pear half and press the top with your fingers to fan out the slices. Transfer to the tart, placing the fruit on the filling like spokes of a wheel. If you like, remove a few slices from each half before arranging and use to fill in any gaps in the center.

4 Place the tart on the hot baking sheet and bake for 50–55 minutes, or until the filling is set and well browned. Cool on a wire rack.

5 ▼ Meanwhile, heat the brandy or water and the jam in a small saucepan, then brush over the top of the hot tart to glaze. Serve the tart at room temperature.

DESSERTS

Simple and wholesome homemade desserts are the hallmark of country cooking. They are usually made from local ingredients – apples in Normandy, cherries in the central regions, peaches and pears further south, and prunes from Agen, in the southwest. In French homes, especially in the country, weekday desserts are often nothing fancier than fresh fruit and cheese, but family occasions and other celebrations provide the opportunity for more festive fare – custards or crêpes perhaps, or an apple charlotte. These kinds of traditional rustic desserts prepared in family kitchens and provincial restaurants are wonderfully satisfying and appealing in their simplicity.

CRÊPES WITH ORANGE SAUCE

Crêpes Suzette

This is one of the best known French desserts and is easy to do at home. You can make the crêpes in advance; then you will be able to put the dish together quickly at the last minute.

SERVES 6

⅔ cup flour
¼ tsp salt
2 tbsp superfine sugar
2 eggs, lightly beaten
1 cup milk
4 tbsp water
2 tbsp orange flower water or orange liqueur (optional)
2 tbsp unsalted butter, melted, plus more for frying

FOR THE ORANGE SAUCE
6 tbsp unsalted butter
¼ cup superfine sugar
grated zest and juice of 1 large orange
grated zest and juice of 1 lemon
⅔ cup fresh orange juice
4 tbsp orange liqueur, plus more for flaming (optional)
brandy, for flaming (optional)
orange segments, to decorate

1 ▲ In a medium bowl, sift together the flour, salt and sugar. Make a well in the center and pour in the beaten eggs. Using an electric whisk, beat the eggs, adding a little flour until it is all incorporated. Slowly whisk in the milk and water to make a smooth batter. Whisk in the orange flower water or liqueur, if using, then strain the batter into a large pitcher and set aside for 20–30 minutes. If the batter thickens, add a little milk or water to thin.

2 ▲ Heat a 7–8 inch crêpe pan (preferably nonstick) over medium heat. Stir the melted butter into the crêpe batter. Brush the hot pan with a little extra melted butter and pour in about 2 tbsp of the batter. Quickly tilt and rotate the pan to cover the base with a thin layer of batter. Cook for about 1 minute until the top is set and the base is golden. With a spatula, lift the edge to check the color, then carefully turn over the crêpe and cook for 20–30 seconds, just to set. Slide the crêpe out onto a plate.

3 ▲ Continue cooking the crêpes, stirring the batter occasionally and brushing the pan with a little melted butter as and when necessary. Place a sheet of wax paper between each crêpe as they are stacked to prevent sticking. (Crêpes can be prepared ahead to this point – wrap and chill until ready to use.)

4 To make the sauce, melt the butter in a large frying pan over medium-low heat, then stir in the sugar, orange and lemon zest and juice, the additional orange juice and the orange liqueur.

5 ▲ Place a crêpe in the pan browned-side down, swirling gently to coat with the sauce. Fold it in half, then in half again to form a triangle and push to the side of the pan. Continue heating and folding the crêpes until all are warm and covered with the sauce.

6 ▲ To flame the crêpes, heat 2–3 tbsp each of orange liqueur and brandy in a small saucepan over medium heat. Remove the pan from the heat, carefully ignite the liquid with a match then gently pour over the crêpes. Scatter over the orange segments and serve at once.

BAKED CARAMEL CUSTARD

Crème Caramel

Also called crème renversée, *this is one of the most popular French desserts and is wonderful when freshly made. This is a slightly lighter version of the traditional recipe.*

SERVES 6–8

1¼ cups granulated sugar
4 tbsp water
1 vanilla bean or 2 tsp vanilla extract
1¾ cups milk
1 cup heavy cream
5 large eggs
2 egg yolks

1 Put ⅞ cup of the sugar in a small heavy saucepan with the water to moisten. Bring to a boil over high heat, swirling the pan to dissolve the sugar. Boil, without stirring, until the syrup turns a dark caramel color (this will take about 4–5 minutes).

2 ▼ Immediately pour the caramel into a 4 cup soufflé dish. If it is hot, hold the dish with oven mitts, before quickly swirling the dish to coat the base and sides with the caramel and set aside. (The caramel will harden quickly as it cools.) Place the dish in a small roasting pan.

3 ▲ Preheat the oven to 325°F. With a small sharp knife, carefully split the vanilla bean lengthwise and scrape the black seeds into a medium saucepan. Add the milk and cream and bring just to a boil over medium-high heat, stirring frequently. Remove the pan from the heat, cover and set aside for 15–20 minutes.

4 In a bowl, whisk the eggs and egg yolks with the remaining sugar for 2–3 minutes until smooth and creamy. Whisk in the hot milk and carefully strain the mixture into the caramel-lined dish. Cover with foil.

5 Place the dish in a roasting pan and pour in enough boiling water to come halfway up the side of the dish. Bake the custard for 40–45 minutes until a knife inserted about 2 inches from the edge comes out clean (the custard should be just set). Remove from the roasting pan and cool for at least ½ hour, then chill overnight.

6 To turn out, carefully run a sharp knife around the edge of the dish to loosen the custard. Cover the dish with a serving plate and, holding them tightly, invert the dish and plate together. Gently lift one edge of the dish, allowing the caramel to run over the sides, then slowly lift off the dish.

CHOCOLATE CREAM PUFFS

Profiteroles au Chocolat

This mouth-watering dessert is served in cafés throughout France. Sometimes the cream puffs are filled with whipped cream instead of ice cream, but they are always drizzled with chocolate sauce.

<u>SERVES 4–6</u>

10 ounces semisweet chocolate
8 tbsp warm water
3 cups vanilla ice cream
FOR THE CREAM PUFFS
¾ cup flour
¼ tsp salt
pinch of ground nutmeg
¾ cup water
6 tbsp unsalted butter, cut into
   6 pieces
3 eggs

1 Preheat the oven to 400°F and lightly butter a large baking sheet.

2 To make the profiteroles, sift together the flour, salt and nutmeg. In a medium saucepan, bring the water and butter to a boil. Remove from the heat and add the dry ingredients all at once. Beat with a wooden spoon for about 1 minute until well blended and the mixture starts to pull away from the sides of the pan, then set the pan over a low heat and cook the mixture for about 2 minutes, beating constantly. Remove from the heat.

3 ▲ Beat 1 egg in a small bowl and set aside. Add the remaining eggs, one at a time, to the flour mixture, beating well after each. Add the beaten egg by teaspoonfuls until the dough is smooth and shiny; it should pull away and fall slowly when dropped from a spoon.

4 ▼ Using a tablespoon, drop the dough onto the baking sheet in 12 mounds. Bake for 25–30 minutes until the pastry is well risen and browned. Turn off the oven and leave the puffs to cool with the oven door open.

5 To make the sauce, place the chocolate and water in a double-boiler or in a bowl placed over a pan of hot water and let melt, stirring occasionally. Keep warm until ready to serve, or reheat, over simmering water.

6 Split the cream puffs in half and put a small scoop of ice cream in each. Arrange on a serving platter or divide among individual plates. Pour the chocolate sauce over the top and serve at once.

GINGER BAKED PEARS
Poires au Gingembre

This simple dessert is the kind that would be served after Sunday lunch or a family supper. Try to find Comice or Anjou pears – the recipe is especially useful for slightly underripe fruit.

<u>SERVES 4</u>

4 large pears
1¼ cups heavy cream
¼ cup superfine sugar
½ tsp vanilla extract
¼ tsp ground cinnamon
pinch of ground nutmeg
1 tsp grated gingerroot

VARIATION

If desired, you could substitute about 1 tbsp finely chopped ginger preserved in syrup for the fresh gingerroot and add a little of the ginger syrup to the cream.

---

1 Preheat the oven to 375°F. Lightly butter a large shallow baking dish.

2 ▼ Peel the pears, cut them in half lengthwise using a large sharp knife and remove the cores. Arrange, cut-sides down, in a single layer in the baking dish.

3 ▲ Mix together the cream, sugar, vanilla extract, cinnamon, nutmeg and ginger and pour over the pears.

4 Bake for 30–35 minutes, basting from time to time, until the pears are tender and browned on top and the cream is thick and bubbly. Cool slightly before serving.

PRUNES POACHED IN RED WINE
Compôte de Pruneaux Agennaise

Serve this simple dessert on its own, or with crème fraîche or vanilla ice cream. The most delicious plump prunes come from the orchards around Agen in Southwest France.

<u>SERVES 8–10</u>

1 orange
1 lemon
3 cups fruity red wine
2 cups water
¼ cup superfine sugar, or to taste
1 cinnamon stick
pinch of freshly grated nutmeg
2 or 3 cloves
1 tsp black peppercorns
1 bay leaf
2 pounds large pitted prunes, soaked in cold water
strips of orange rind, to decorate

1 Using a vegetable peeler, peel two or three strips of rind from both the orange and lemon. Squeeze the juice from both and put in a large saucepan.

2 Add the wine, water, sugar, spices, peppercorns, bay leaf and strips of rind to the pan.

3 ▲ Bring to a boil over a medium heat, stirring occasionally to dissolve the sugar. Drain the prunes and add to the saucepan, reduce the heat to low and simmer, covered, for 10–15 minutes until the prunes are tender. Remove from the heat and set aside until cool.

4 ▼ Using a slotted spoon, transfer the prunes to a serving dish. Return the cooking liquid to medium-high heat and bring to a boil. Boil for 5–10 minutes until slightly reduced and syrupy, then pour or strain over the prunes. Cool, then chill before serving, decorated with strips of orange rind, if you like.

GLOSSARY

The following terms are frequently used in French cooking. In the recipes we have tried to reduce the use of technical terms by describing the procedures, but understanding these words is helpful.

BAIN-MARIE: a baking pan or dish set in a roasting pan or saucepan of water. It allows the food to cook indirectly and protects delicate foods; a double boiler is also a kind of water bath, or *bain-marie*.

BAKE BLIND: to bake or part-bake a pastry shell before adding a filling, usually done to prevent the filling making the pastry soggy.

BASTE: to moisten food with fat or cooking juices while it is cooking.

BEURRE MANIÉ: equal parts of butter and flour blended to a paste and whisked into simmering cooking liquid for thickening after cooking is completed.

BLANCH: to immerse vegetables and sometimes fruit in boiling water in order to loosen skin, remove bitterness or saltiness or preserve color.

BOIL: to keep liquid at a temperature producing bubbles that break the surface.

BOUQUET GARNI: a bunch of herbs, usually including a bay leaf, thyme sprigs and parsley stalks, used to impart flavor during cooking, often tied for easy removal.

CLARIFY: to make an opaque liquid clear and remove impurities; stocks are clarified using egg white, butter by skimming.

COULIS: a purée, usually fruit or vegetable, sometimes sweetened or flavored with herbs, but not thickened, used as a sauce.

CROÛTONS: small crisp pieces of fried or baked crustless bread.

DEGLAZE: to dissolve the sediment from the bottom of a cooking pan by adding liquid and bringing to a boil, stirring. This is then used as the basis for a sauce or gravy.

DEGREASE: to remove fat from cooking liquid, either by spooning off after it has risen to the top or by chilling until the fat is congealed and lifting it off.

DICE: to cut food into square uniform pieces about ¼in.

EMULSIFY: to combine two usually incompatible ingredients until smooth by mixing rapidly while slowly adding one to the other so they are held in suspension.

FOLD: to combine ingredients, using a large rubber spatula or metal spoon, by cutting down through the center of the bowl, then along the side and up to the top in a semicircular motion; it is important not to deflate or over-work ingredients while folding.

FOOD MILL *(mouli-légumes)*: tool for puréeing found in most French kitchens which strains as it purées.

GLAZE: to coat food with a sweet or savory mixture producing a shiny surface when set.

GRATINÉ: to give a browned, crisp surface to a baked dish.

HERBES DE PROVENCE: a mixture of aromatic dried herbs, which grow wild in Provence, usually thyme, marjoram, oregano and summer savory.

INFUSE: to extract flavor by steeping in hot liquid.

JULIENNE: thin matchstick pieces of vegetables, fruit or other food.

MACERATE: to bathe fruit in liquid to soften and flavor it.

PAPILLOTE: a greased non-stick baking paper or foil parcel, traditionally heart-shaped, enclosing food for cooking.

PARBOIL: to partially cook food by boiling.

POACH: to cook food, submerged in liquid, by gentle simmering.

REDUCE: to boil a liquid for the purpose of concentrating the flavor by evaporation.

ROUX: a cooked mixture of fat and flour used to thicken liquids such as soups, stews and sauces.

SAUTÉ: to fry quickly in a small amount of fat over a high heat.

SCALD: to heat liquid, usually milk, until bubbles begin to form around the edge.

SCORE: to make shallow incisions to aid penetration of heat or liquid or for decoration.

SIMMER: to keep a liquid at just below boiling point so the liquid just trembles.

SKIM: to remove froth or scum from the surface of stocks etc.

STEAM: moist heat cooking method by which vaporized liquid cooks food in a closed container.

SWEAT: to cook gently in fat, covered, so liquid in ingredients is rendered to steam them.

INDEX

A

Almonds:
pear and almond cream
tart, 83
spiced-nut palmiers, 79
Alsatian leek and onion
tartlets, 36
Anchovies:
Provençal salad, 16
steak with anchovy
sauce, 66
Apples:
apple Charlotte, 87
apple tart, 82

B

Bacon:
cheese and bacon quiche, 35
curly endive salad with
bacon, 15
lentils with bacon, 28
Baked caramel custard, 90
Batter:
cherry batter pudding, 86
Beef:
Burgundy beef stew, 64
steak with anchovy
sauce, 66
Boeuf bourguignon, 64
Bouillabaisse, 44
Braised red cabbage, 29
Bread:
apple Charlotte, 87
Brioches, individual, 77
Brittany butter cookies, 78
Brussels sprouts:
festive Brussels
sprouts, 20
Burgundy beef stew, 64

C

Cabbage:
braised red cabbage, 29
guinea hen with cabbage, 59
sauerkraut with pork and
sausages, 70
Cakes:
French chocolate cake, 81
pound cake with red
fruit, 76
Cannellini beans:
Toulouse cassoulet, 71
Caramel:
baked caramel custard, 90
Casseroles and stews:
Burgundy beef stew, 64
casseroled rabbit with
thyme, 58
duck stew with olives, 61

Mediterranean fish stew, 44
Cassoulet, 71
Cauliflower au gratin, 21
*Champignons sauvages à la
bordelaise*, 22
Charlotte aux pommes, 87
Cheese:
Alsatian leek and onion
tartlets, 36
cauliflower au gratin, 21
cheese and bacon quiche, 35
cheese and ham
croissants, 32
cheese and onion flan, 34
cheese puff ring, 32
twice-baked soufflés, 38
Cherries:
cherry batter pudding, 86
pound cake with red
fruit, 76
Chestnuts:
festive Brussels sprouts, 20
Chicken:
chicken chasseur, 55
chicken with garlic, 54
chicken with morels, 52
old-fashioned chicken
fricassée, 56
Chocolate:
chocolate cream puffs, 91
French chocolate cake, 81
Chou rouge braisé, 29
Choucroûte garnie, 70
Choufleur au gratin, 21
*Choux de Bruxelles
braisées*, 20
Choux pastry:
cheese puff ring, 32
chocolate cream puffs, 91
Clafoutis aux cerises, 86
Cod with lentils and leeks, 47
*Compôte de pruneaux
agennaise*, 92
Cookies:
Brittany butter cookies, 78
*Coquilles Saint Jacques au
gratin*, 42
*Coquilles Saint Jacques
meunières*, 48
Country-style pâté with
leeks, 72
Crêpes Suzettes, 88
Crêpes with orange sauce, 88
Crème caramel, 90
Croissants:
cheese and ham croissants, 32
*croissants au fromage et
jambon*, 32
Croûtons, 16
Curly endive salad with
bacon, 15

D

Desserts:
apple Charlotte, 87
baked caramel custard, 90
cherry batter pudding, 86
crêpes with orange sauce, 88
ginger baked pears, 92
prunes poached in red
wine, 92
Duck stew with olives, 61

E

Eggs:
Provençal salad, 16
*Entrecôte au beurre
d'anchois*, 66

F

Faisan rôti au porto, 60
Festive Brussels sprouts, 20
Fish:
cod with lentils and
leeks, 47
Mediterranean fish stew, 44
potato-topped baked
fish, 46
Provençal salad, 16
Flamiche au fromage, 34
French chocolate cake, 81
French onion soup, 10
French scalloped
potatoes, 25
Fricassée de lapin au thym, 58
Fricassée de poulet, 56
Frisée aux lardons, 15
*Fruits de mer à la
provençale*, 48

G

Garlic:
baked tomatoes with
garlic, 26
chicken with garlic, 54
croûtons, 16
garlic mashed potatoes, 24
garlicky scallops and
shrimp, 48
Garlic sausage:
potato salad with
sausage, 14
Gâteau au chocolat, 81
Gigot farci, 68
Ginger baked pears, 92
Gougère, 32
Green beans:
Provençal salad, 16
Guinea hen with
cabbage, 59

H

Ham:
cheese and ham croissants, 32
Haricot beans:
Toulouse cassoulet, 71
Hazelnuts:
spiced-nut palmiers, 79

K

Kidneys:
roast stuffed lamb, 68
veal kidneys with
mustard, 67

L

Lamb:
roast stuffed lamb, 68
Toulouse cassoulet, 71
Leeks:
Alsatian leek and onion
tartlets, 36
cod with lentils and
leeks, 47
country-style pâté with
leeks, 72
Lemon tart, 80
*Lentilles braisées aux
lardons*, 28
Lentils:
cod with lentils and
leeks, 47
lentils with bacon, 28

M

Mediterranean fish
stew, 44
Morels:
chicken with morels, 52
*Morue aux lentilles et
poireaux*, 47
Moules à la crème, 43
Moules marinière, 43
Mushrooms:
chicken chasseur, 55
chicken with morels, 52
sautéed wild
mushrooms, 22
scallops with
mushrooms, 42
wild mushroom soup, 11
Mussels:
mussels steamed in white
wine, 43
mussels with cream
sauce, 43
Mustard:
veal kidneys with
mustard, 67

N

Nuts:
spiced-nut palmiers, 79

O

Old-fashioned chicken
fricassée, 56
Olives:
duck stew with olives, 61
Provençal salad, 16
Onions:
Alsatian leek and onion
tartlets, 36
cheese and onion flan, 34
French onion soup, 10
Oranges:
crêpes with orange sauce, 88

P

Palmiers, 79
Pastries:
spiced-nut palmiers, 79
Pâté:
country-style pâté with
leeks, 72
pâté de porc aux poireaux, 72
Pears:
ginger baked pears, 92
pear and almond cream
tart, 83
spiced pear tart, 82
Petites brioches, 77
Petits gâteaux bretons, 78
Pheasant:
roast pheasant with port, 60
Pintade au chou, 59
Poires au gingembre, 92
Poisson au Suquet, 46
Pommes de terre
dauphinoises, 25
Pork:
country-style pâté with
leeks, 72
sauerkraut with pork and
sausages, 70
Toulouse cassoulet, 71
Potatoes:
French scalloped
potatoes, 25
garlic mashed potatoes, 24
potato salad with
sausage, 14
potato-topped baked
fish, 46
Provençal salad, 16
Poulet à l'ail, 54
Poulet sauté chasseur, 55
Pound cake with red fruit, 76
Profiteroles au chocolat, 91
Provençal salad, 16
Provençal vegetable soup, 12

Prunes poached in red
wine, 92
Purée de pommes de terre à
l'ail, 24

Q

Quatre quarts aux fruits, 76
Quiche:
cheese and bacon quiche, 35

R

Rabbit:
casseroled rabbit with
thyme, 58
Ragoût de canard aux olives, 61
Raspberries:
pound cake with red
fruit, 76
Red cabbage:
braised red cabbage, 29
Rice pilaf, 22
Roast stuffed lamb, 68

S

Salad:
curly endive salad with
bacon, 15
potato salad with
sausage, 14
Provençal salad, 16

Salade de pommes de terre, 14
Salade niçoise, 16
Sauerkraut with pork and
sausages, 70
Sausages:
Toulouse cassoulet, 71
Scallops:
garlicky scallops and
shrimp, 48
sautéed scallops, 48
scallops with
mushrooms, 42
Shrimp:
garlicky scallops and
shrimp, 48
Soufflés:
soufflés renversés, 38
twice-baked soufflés, 38
Soup:
French onion soup, 10
Provençal vegetable
soup, 12
wild mushroom soup, 11
Soupe au pistou, 12
Spiced-nut palmiers, 79
Spiced pear tart, 82
Steak with anchovy
sauce, 66
Strawberries:
pound cake with red
fruit, 76
Suprêmes de volaille farcies aux
morilles, 52

T

Tarte au citron, 80
Tarte aux poires frangipane, 83
Tarte aux pommes, 82
Tartlettes alsaciennes, 36
Tarts and flans:
Alsatian leek and onion
tartlets, 36
apple tart, 82
lemon tart, 80
pear and almond cream
tart, 83
spiced pear tart, 82
Thyme:
casseroled rabbit with
thyme, 58
Tian Provençal, 26
Tomates à la provençale, 26
Tomatoes:
baked tomatoes with
garlic, 26
chicken chasseur, 55
twice-baked soufflés, 38
zucchini and tomato
bake, 26
Toulouse cassoulet, 71
Twice-baked soufflés, 38

V

Veal kidneys with
mustard, 67
Vegetables:
Provençal vegetable
soup, 12
Velouté de champignons
sauvages, 11

W

Walnuts:
spiced-nut palmiers, 79
Wild mushrooms:
chicken with morels, 52
sautéed wild
mushrooms, 22
wild mushroom soup, 11

Y

Yeast cakes:
individual brioches, 77

Z

Zucchini and tomato bake, 26